A LADY'S DIARY

A LADY'S DIARY

BEFORE AND DURING THE INDIAN MUTINY

M. H. OUVRY

GYAN

Published by

GYAN

Gyan Publishing House
5, Ansari Road
Daryaganj, New Delhi-110002
Phone: 011-47034999, 9811692060
E-mail: books@gyanbooks.com

Distribution Network
gyanbooks.com
India, USA, Canada, UK, Australia

ISBN: 978-93-6780-134-5 (PB)

First Published, 1892

2nd Impression 2024

Printed at: Gyan Press, Delhi.

**A LADY'S DIARY:
BEFORE AND DURING THE INDIAN MUTINY**

Author: M. H. OUVRY

A LADY'S DIARY

A Lady's Diary

Before and During the Indian Mutiny.

BY

M. H. OUVRY.

LYMINGTON:
PRINTED BY CHAS. T. KING.
1892.

PREFACE.

I HAVE often been asked to publish my DIARY, as containing much that is interesting concerning the period of that terrible crisis in our Indian history, but hitherto I have not had resolution enough to do so. Now, however, that upwards of thirty years have elapsed since it was written, and my husband has printed his "Cavalry Experiences," I venture, with great diffidence, to give my Indian Diary to the public.

I fear many of the details will not be generally interesting: but to those mentioned in it, it may recall to their memory events perhaps long forgotten, and may also interest the descendants or relations of those who have since passed away.

There are no pretensions in this Diary to literary merit, and I trust all errors in style or composition will be pardoned; with very few alterations and omissions, it is word for word as I wrote it; and, although I feel that a Diary cannot fail to be somewhat egotistical, I have neither the time nor perhaps the ability to re-write it in another form.

I have not touched upon any of the causes of the Indian Mutiny, feeling incompetent to enter into a subject which has been so ably treated by many writers. It was a terrible time to have been in India, although, happily, I did not personally suffer any of the horrors of it.

It may be noticed, that in speaking of Regiments, I have styled them "Queens" when mentioning the 32nd Regiment of Foot, the 52nd Light Infantry, etc. In the days of old "John Company" people were in the habit of distinguishing them by calling them "Queens" or "Company's," titles which would not be understood in these days, when the Honorable East India Company has ceased to exist.

I have included our voyages to and from India; the first, round the Cape in a sailing-vessel; the latter, by the so-called overland route, as both modes are now things of the past, and may therefore be interesting from that point of view.

M. H. OUVRY.

THE SALTERNS,
LYMINGTON, HANTS.
November, 1892.

A Lady's Diary

BEFORE AND DURING THE INDIAN MUTINY.

WE were married in January 1854, my husband being a Captain in the 3rd King's Own Light Dragoons (afterwards Hussars). The regiment was then quartered at Exeter, but when we returned from our wedding trip, my husband's troop had been sent to Dorchester, where we remained about two months, when the 3rd received its orders for Manchester, about the middle of May. The regiment marched in three detachments, I rode on horseback at the head of one detachment through Sherborne to Milbourne Port—where Sir Wm. Meddlycott called and invited Henry and myself to his house—thence to Shepton Mallet, where we remained over Sunday; then to Keynsham; next day to Gloucester; then on to Tewkesbury, Worcester, etc., being billetted at the different hotels, and I enjoyed the trip very much.

We took a small unfurnished house at Manchester, but were only in it eighteen days when H's troop was ordered to Burnley to make room for the Scotch Greys, who were to stay at Manchester until the *Himalaya* arrived at Liverpool to take them to Turkey for the Crimean War. Two days' march brought us to Burnley, staying one night at Rochdale. The barracks are a mile from the town and no lodgings to be found, so after staying two or three days with the clergyman, I went into barracks for the first and only time in my life and enjoyed the novelty very much.

In September, my husband purchased his Majority in the 3rd Light Dragoons and then exchanged into the 9th Lancers which were stationed at Umballah, where my brother John's regiment was also quartered. We left England on the 7th of November 1854, in the Aberdeen clipper-built ship *Omar Pasha* (her first voyage), it being too late in the season for any of Green's ships. We had very few passengers, principally officers going to join their regiments in India.

Wednesday, 8th. We anchored in the Downs for the night, but early on the 9th, a favourable breeze springing up, we set sail and had soon passed the Isle of Wight, where the pilot left us. I felt unwell for the first few days, but was not regularly sea-sick, and by the 13th was feeling quite well again. We had by this time got into such lovely warm weather, and were able to enjoy cold salt water baths every morning.

Wednesday, 15th. We passed a French ship. At half-past two a squall came on, and we had rough weather.

Thursday, 16th. We passed a fearful night, the ship rolled and tossed so much I scarcely slept at all, and the captain did not go to bed. We passed Madeira early this morning, and later the Desertas, some rocks at a little distance from the Island; they looked so pretty, the light playing upon and tinting them with such a variety of colours. The very air seems different here to anything I have ever felt before —so beautifully soft and yet fresh.

Sunday, 19th. Mr. Hart* was to have read prayers to-day but he was not well. We saw land again—one of the Canary Islands.

*29th Queen's Regiment.

Wednesday, 22nd. Yesterday and to-day we saw a ship, quite an event in the monotony of a long voyage. A little while after, we passed through such a lovely phosphorescent sea; now we see flying fish, and some actually came on board, they are very small.

Thursday, 23rd. Passed the Cape Verde Islands, but not near enough to see them.

Friday, 24th. The weather has become very warm now—thermometer 82° and 83°. We saw another ship, an English one. We sail so fast we generally pass them in a very short time.

Sunday, 26th. Mr. Hart read the service in the saloon with the thermometer at 84°. We had some regular tropical rain.

Monday, 27th. A wet morning. We were becalmed almost the whole day and the weather was intensely hot. Mr. White went up the rigging to the mizen royal. In the evening there was such beautiful summer lightning. We tried to cool some lemonade by putting the bottle into the sea attached to a long rope—it sank to a good depth but came up quite warm. H. bought two dozen lemonade for me at Gravesend and now we find that only five or six of the bottles at the top are lemonade all the rest being soda water. I daresay it is a trick often practised, with impunity, on those going abroad. H. left his little portmanteau at the hotel at Gravesend, containing his hair brushes, silver shaving apparatus out of his dressing case, and some linen. It was very careless of the people at the hotel.

Tuesday, 28th. We met a homeward bound vessel, we therefore lay-to, and she soon came towards us. We got all our letters ready and a boat was lowered, but it took two or three men, a quarter of an hour baling, to keep the water under; then the captain, mate, H. and three other passengers got in, taking off their shoes. They had to bale out the water the whole way to the ship which was about two miles off, but it gradually came nearer. Our boat returned with the captain of the other ship and our own, also a Lieutenant Chapman, who was returning to England with his mother. The ship was the *Ratcliffe,* from the Mauritius and had only been forty-five days out. We gave her some of our potatoes and she sent us a present of some claret. The *Ratcliffe's* passengers had been on board another vessel in the morning, which had left England thirty nine days ago, while the *Omar Pasha* has only been out twenty. The gentlemen dined on board the *Ratcliffe,* and when they left it, the two ships were close together. Their sailors gave three loud cheers which were soon answered by ours. They returned them and set sail for England.

In the evening, our sailors sent off a tar-barrel, and Neptune is to come on board on Saturday.

Thursday, 30th. Neptune's secretary came on a donkey, made up for the occasion, to take down the names of those who have never crossed the line.

[*December,* 1854.]

Saturday, 2nd. Neptune and his wife came in a kind of car covered with sheep skins, and there was a procession with a drum and fifes. Amphitrite, one of the sailors dressed up as a woman, really looked like a very rough peasant girl; both were very much painted. After a little parade, they went to work and played all manner of tricks on the sailors that had not before crossed the line, poking tar and pitch into their mouths, and making them smell a bottle with a cork in it in which there were sharp nails, the victims being all the time blindfolded; the finale was tossing them head over heels into a sail full of water. One of the gentlemen, Mr Hart, who was amusing himself playing the hose on them, first got a pail of water thrown over him, and afterwards was pushed from his high seat, head foremost into the sail of water, much to his indignation.

We crossed the line at 10 o'clock on Sunday.

Thursday, 7th. We have gone 20° 25^{m} in five days since we crossed the line.

Friday, 8th. The least thing is an event on board ship, even the sighting of three rocks, about 30 miles from Trinidad. We saw some grampuses, they were at first taken for whales as they throw up waterspouts in the same way that whales do.

Saturday, 16th. At half-past twelve a gale began, the sea rose, and we had a very uncomfortable day.

Sunday, 17th. A most unpleasant night and day, we could not have service. I went up on deck but the spray dashed over me and I got wet through.

Monday, 18th. The gale was over to-day at about twelve o'clock, but the sea continued very rough. We had nothing but a sea-pie for dinner, which is served up in a soup tureen. It is made of all kinds of meat and poultry with pudding crust swimming about in it; not at all bad eating. Mr. Edwards fell down on deck and afterwards found he had broken his collar-bone. The boatswain is very ill indeed, and the doctor does not think he can live more than two or three days. He took a great fancy to drink lemonade but there was none on board, so I gave him the few bottles I had.

Thursday, 21st. This morning the head of the mainmast was found to be sprung, most likely in the gale, and we have been rolling dreadfully ever since.

Saturday, 23rd. We had a good squall this evening which sent us on capitally. We went to the top of the companion ladder to look at it. The mizen topmast broke to-day.

Sunday, 24th. A great deal of pitching, tossing, and rolling, and the day was rainy and miserable.

Monday, 25th. Christmas Day. Mr. Hart read the service. The boatswain is getting well, to every one's surprise.

Tuesday, 26th. The mizen topmast was nearly ready to be put up when the carpenter drove a chisel into his thigh which will delay matters, and lay him up for a day or two. However, it was put up the next day very easily.

Friday, 29th. The mainmast was put up to-day. The captain was on deck from five in the morning until ten at night, and even had his meals on deck. It was a long concern getting the mast up and then there were all the sails and rigging to be put in order. I went on the forecastle to see some porpoises which were crossing in front of the ship. H. was going to try and harpoon some, but by the time the instrument was ready they were gone. And so ended the year 1854.

[*January*, 1855.]

Monday, 1st. A fine day but rather cold. We are not going on very fast. H. has made a bet of ten rupees with Mr. Hart that we shall reach Bombay in January. Mr. Hart thinks we shall not arrive before February. Mr. Cooper was pulling at a rope, and in some way got his hand in the pulley, two of his fingers being very much hurt.

All this first week of January we have made very little progress, having hardly any wind. We had a very prosperous beginning, but I am afraid we are going to pay for it now. Four shots were fired from two little cannons, they made a great noise and shook the whole ship. H. amused himself by knocking down, with his rifle, six bottles hung up on one of the yards.

Tuesday, 9th. A homeward bound ship in sight. We lay to as we had no wind, but she fought shy of us, either did not know the ship, being a new one, or thought we wanted something. Mr. Hart went over the stern to pick up part of a chair that Mr. Edwards had thrown over-board, and got covered with paint! The weather has become dreadfully hot, just as at home they are having the greatest cold, probably with snow on the ground. All the sherry is finished, also the nuts, almonds, jam etc., and almost everything appears to be running short. We have hitherto had champagne twice a week.

Monday, 15th. We saw a number of 'boatswains' or as the French call them *paille-en-queue*, they are very pretty birds, generally white, with a long feather in their tail, hence their French name. A number of albacore were playing round the ship, jumping to such a height to catch the flying-fish which abound.

Tuesday, 16th. We caught a small shark about nine feet long, it did not make much resistance. We tasted some of it, and I think I might have been able to eat it if I had not known it was shark!

Thursday, 18th. While we were sitting at breakfast, we heard a call for the life-buoy. Every person rushed on deck;

there were two men overboard. Some sailors jumped into the sea and managed to save one, but the other was drowned. H. saw him sinking through forty feet of water, most likely he had knocked his head in falling. It appears that some part of the rigging or mast had given way, and these men went up to mend it; their united weight was too much, and the top-gallant mast giving way, two of them were thrown into the sea. They tried to cling to the side of the ship—it was calm, and we were not going on at all—but the ship was rolling so terribly that they went an immense way under water every time she rolled. If there had only been a boat the poor man might have been saved. The other man was almost exhausted before they got him on board, and he had first fallen on the rail and injured his collar-bone. The adventure gave such a feeling of gloom to the whole day.

Saturday, 20th. Thermometer at 90° in the shade and 125° in the sun. There was a cry of land! some went up the rigging, others on the forecastle. The captain did not think there was any land in that directon, and indeed it turned out to be a cloud. We have most beautiful sunsets.

Tuesday, 23rd. A great many birds about, which shows that we are not very far from land. The sailors caught a bird, a "noddy," I believe, it is called; it escaped, but soon came back to be caught again. H. played three games of chess with Mr. Edgeworth, the latter won two, giving H. any piece he liked, except the queen. In the evening we saw a whale; after spouting, it rose partly out of the water.

Wednesday, 24th. A calm, and very hot. There was an auction in the evening to sell the property of the poor man who was drowned.

Friday, 26th. Squally, with calms between the squalls, the latter send us on nicely.

Sunday, 28th. Violent rain all night, accompanied by the most vivid lightning I ever saw, the thunder was not loud. The cook made us a cake last night. I just tasted it, and put it on the window-sill looking on to the lower deck; but, while we were both in the cabin, someone managed to crawl in and steal it!

The wind is contrary; we are going east, and cannot make the one degree of latitude we want of the line. I believe we have not made any latitude for five days.

The deck is being caulked, which makes a great noise, and will take four or five days to complete.

[*February*, 1855.]

Friday, 2nd. We tack twice in twenty four hours, only gaining one point north each way. From twelve o'clock yesterday to twelve to-day we went two hundred and fifty miles, only thirty of which was on our course!

Friday, 9th. A dead calm all last night and to-day. Someone has stolen the chess board, so we cannot play any more; it belongs to Mr. Hart.

There was a tremendous row on board, the monotony of the voyage is trying to peoples' tempers.

Saturday, 10th. Land was smelt this morning and some said they saw it before the sun rose. There were some water spouts seen.

We saw two ships, one of which the captain, H., Mr. Hart and Mr. Edgeworth went on board. They had no idea it was so far off or they would not have gone; it was nine miles, and the captain of that ship thought they were shipwrecked mariners come off from some island, until they came on board and said they had come from the ship whose topsails only were visible. However in four or five hours we had got close to each other. The captain was exceedingly kind, giving us a goose, turkey, etc., etc. He had left Cochin only the day before, and gave us the first news we had had since leaving England, all about the Crimean war.

Sunday, 11th. This morning at half-past five, we saw land, the Ghât mountains. We coasted along the shore at a distance of about fifteen miles; at last, we came in sight of a small town and harbour, when the captain ran our ship in to within five or six miles of the land. Some native boats came off to us, and Mr. Edgeworth, Mr. D' Aubigné, (a midshipman,) and Mr Ryder, went on shore in one of them. The captain, Mr Edwards, H. and myself went in the ship's boat, Mr and Mrs Cooper and the second mate in the dinghy. It was delightful setting foot on land after ninety two days on board ship. We asked for the governor, but they took us to a clergyman of the Church of Scotland, who, with his wife and sister-in-law, was very kind, and gave us a very nice luncheon. I think their name was Whitehouse. They had only arrived from England about ten days previously, which they left in July in the *Seringapatam,* an old ship which broke down, and they were obliged to stay for three months at the Mauritius until they could get another ship. At half-past six, we left Cochin, having stayed there about two hours. The captain bought all kinds of things, turkeys, prawns, (very fine) a monkey and a quantity of bread. The trees looked so beautifully green and fresh, not so the grass which was very brown and parched, affording very poor food to some miserable looking little cows and goats. I saw a very pretty little black boy dressed in a pink frock and trousers in one, the usual dress of children in India, except the common natives, whose children are generally quite naked, the men only having a piece of calico round their middle and another piece wound round their head. They talk a kind of jargon and few could understand H's Hindoostanee.

The Coopers, with the second mate, not appearing, we were all much alarmed as there is a sand bank near, so the captain sent the other boat to look after them. They were met returning in a native boat their own having got upon the sand bank close to the shore, and nearly filled with water; with great difficulty they got back and hired a native canoe. It was nearly eleven o'clock before they returned.

Friday, 16th. Spoke the *Senator* bound for Bombay. one hundred and nine days from Liverpool. She sent a boat to ask for water as she had only eight gallons left. We had none to spare but the captain gave sixty gallons.

Tuesday, 20th. This morning Mrs. Cooper was prematurely confined with a daughter, both doing well however.

Wednesday, 21st. Feb. We had a good wind and got so near Bombay, that a pilot came off and brought us into the harbour at half past six in the evening, after a voyage of one hundred and six days from Gravesend, much longer than we expected. We went at once to the Hope Hall Hotel which we did not reach till nine o'clock, when we had our dinner in a bungalow in the compound, the hotel being full.

My husband had to serve on a court-martial, so we were not able to leave till the 19th of March, by which time the weather had become very hot. The railway is finished as far as Tanna—twenty-four miles. After that we marched up the country, riding on horseback, or sometimes, when tired, travelling in a spring cart drawn by bullocks, where we could lie down and sleep during a night march. We had common carts also drawn by bullocks to carry our luggage, tent, bedding, etc. We used the Dâk bungalow, but very often had our tent pitched half-way when the marches were long.

We met with no adventure on the way, except, one evening, as we were riding along in the dusk, I saw a tiger peering out of the jungle quite close to me; however, before I had time to be frightened, the animal turned and ran away into the jungle. Our little dog Crib began to run after it, but we called him back at once, and so he escaped the fate of H's favorite little dog Sug, which, when he was in India before, was carried off by a *lakra-bagher*, a kind of panther, after having followed H. through the campaign, and been wounded in one of the battles. On another occasion we saw a bear, but it was some distance off.

The roads are, as a rule, very bad, much like a very stony beach. We spent two or three very pleasant days at Gwalior with Major McPherson, the Resident, and reached Agra, where my father was formerly Commandant, on the 12th of May. Of course we had a good look at the celebrated Taj. We remained here till the 15th, when we went by Inland Transit Company to Umballah. We travelled all night andremained during the day at the Dâk bungalows. Twenty-four miles beyond Kurnaul, the road to Umballah is so bad that we had to change into a smaller carriage on two wheels with two horses. It was nearly an hour before we set off again, and after going about half a mile the horses began to kick and bite each other. I thought we should certainly have been upset; then they fell down and plunged, and kicked and bit more violently than ever. At last we got out, the door fortunately being behind, but I scarcely thought myself safe anywhere from those vicious horses. The coachman had been very much bitten by them. We walked back to the Chokee, where the horses are changed, to try and procure fresh ones, and after a long delay we got two others and a fresh carriage, as the other was broken. When we got inside we found the springs of this one were broken and the back part nearly touched the ground, while the front was so high it seemed as if the horses and pole were up in the air. We went on, however, for about a mile, and then came to a full stop, We had five or six men with us and they pushed the wheels and tried to urge on the horses, (they never beat them here, or hardly at all) and got them on about half a dozen yards, when they again stopped and so they went on, stopping every dozen yards, and requiring five minutes before they would go on. At last we saw we should never get to Umballah at this rate, so H. walked two miles back again to the Chokee, and was fortunately able to get two Dhoolies, and bearers, so after a delay of four hours in all, we once more set off, and arrived at Umballah at ten, instead of six, on the morning of the 19th of May, and found the heat and the dust dreadful. We went straight to Colonel Grant* where Mrs. Grant soon had a second breakfast ready for us. They have a nice large bungalow, and with a thermantidote and double punkah, we found it very cool and pleasant. Colonel Grant's nephew, Mr. Frank Grant, lives in a small bungalow in the compound. In the evening we went to hear our band play in some grounds which are being enclosed and laid out for the purpose. The band is to play three times a week.

*The Colonel of the 9th. Lancers, afterwards Sir Hope Grant.

Colonel Grant is Acting Brigadier, as the Brigadier is just now away. H. therefore is in command of the Regiment. After dinner we had some music, Colonel Grant playing on the violoncello, accompanied on the piano by Mrs Grant or on the concertina by his nephew.

Sunday, 20th May. We did not go to church this morning, being scarcely equal, after yesterday's sleepless night, to getting up at half-past four, the service beginning at half-past five; but we went in the evening. The church is only now being built, and service is performed in a Bungalow done up for the purpose; with tatties all along one side, and innumerable punkahs, it was tolerably cool.

Our luggage arrived on the 23rd. Our servants and horses on the 25th, having been only twelve days marching two hundred and fifty miles.

We drive out at five o'clock in the morning, and the Grants and most people dine at four in the hot weather, so as not to curtail the evening drive.

Monday, 28th. We walked out early to the riding-school, and saw a troop knocking with their lances at figures made to resemble men, and jumping over bars. Some of the horses could not be got to go over the bar and backed and reared very much. After breakfast we came to our own house which we have had neatly furnished. In the evening we rode on horseback.

[*June*, 1855.]

Friday, 1st. The Ansons (William Ford's cousins) who are in the hills have lent us their buggy until our carriage is ready. A dust storm came on which prevented our being able to go out.

Sunday, 3rd. A tremendous storm, without rain, last night, which blew down a bees' nest from a tree; they do not make their nest in the hollow of a tree, but fasten their combs to the outside and the bees cluster on it, so that in appearance it only seems like a huge cluster of bees. As soon as it was light the insects flew about, enraged, and at least a hundred of them alighted on one of my poor goats stinging it most dreadfully, its cries were distressing, and in the evening its ears were swollen to three or four inches in thickness, also its tongue, mouth, etc.

Tuesday, 5th. The Brigadier came back to-day, and was saluted with thirteen guns. H. will lose command of the regiment to-morrow. My horse is in hospital with ulcerated mouth, and it will not be well, I am told, for more than a month.

Friday, 8th. H. had to go to a parade this evening, when a soldier was to be flogged for having knocked down a sergeant and thrown a brick at a corporal; he was not sober at the time. He received fifty stripes, and is also to be imprisoned for four months.

Sunday, 10th. This was to have been celebrated as a day of humiliation and intercession on account of the War (with Russia), but very early in the morning, notice was sent round that there would be no service, as an accident had happened to the Church Bungalow. We drove afterwards to see what it was, and found one of the beams of the roof had given way. Weather very hot, thermometer at 9 o'clock in the evening 92°.

Saturday, 16th. Last night, Colonel and Mrs Grant were upset in their buggy. They had driven to Umballah (town) three miles from here, on a very bad road, took no syce or lights with them; it was quite dark when they returned, and they got upset over a heap of kunker, Colonel Grant is laid up having hurt his knee a good deal, and he has had sixty leeches applied to it. Mrs. Grant escaped unhurt; this is the fourth time she has been upset, each time without injury.

Sunday, 17th. Service was performed in the Mess House. It was very cool and pleasant.

Tuesday, 19th. A letter from J.* from Barrackpore in answer to H's written nearly a month ago, asking him to come up and stay with us, he has been ill and only now recovering and "able to do a little tea and toast." The new doctor has been very kind and attentive, taking him to his own house to nurse him. J. says he will try and get leave from the 15th July to 1st Nov.

Wednesday, 27th. This morning it was very hot, thermometer in the room at 92°, outside in the shade 108°. At 5 p.m. a dust-storm came on, gradually the air became cooler, and in half an hour a delicious shower of rain with thunder and lightning, effectually cooled the atmosphere, after which we had a most refreshing drive.

Thursday, 28th. H. went to dine at Mess as usual on Thursdays. I drank tea at the Grants. Colonel Grant was not well enough to go. He is now suffering from the leech bites. A Mr. Currie spent the evening there, he is travelling Dâk from Simla to Delhi and has left his wife at the former place.

[*July*, 1855.]

Monday 2nd. H. brought word that he had seen in the paper the death of Mr. Hart, a Lieutenant in the 29th Queen's, who came out to India in the ship with us.

* My brother, who I had not seen for ten years, his regiment was at Umballah when we left England, but to my great disappointment when we arrived at Bombay, we found it had gone down to Barrackpore, near Calcutta.

Wednesday, 4th. Colonel and Mrs. Grant are going to leave this evening for the hills, as Col. G's leg is very troublesome and does not improve. H. does his duty, and has so much to do that he was not at home till it was almost dark to take me for a ride; I had been ready for more than an hour.

Saturday, 7th. One of the privates of the 9th Lancers was found drowned in a well. He had been missing from the evening of the 5th. The nights are so dark, he must have walked straight in without seeing it.

Monday, 16th. I have not been well and have not been out for ten days. I neither sleep well, nor eat anything, so H. called in the doctor.

Thursday, 19th. H. went to Mess, and Mrs Grant who returned a day or two ago, drank tea with me. I have face-ache which prevents my sleeping. H, sent to Dr Clifford, for something to relieve it, and he gave me morphia, but that made me so ill, and the tic or neuralgic pains in my face have been so severe, that I did not leave my bed till Tuesday, the 24th. Mrs Grant is very kind and comes to see me at least once a day. Dr Clifford visits me twice and sometimes three times in the course of the day. News has come that a mountain tribe has risen and murdered some Europeans (two ladies), and plundered and burnt their Bungalow. The 56th Regiment has been ordered there, so I am afraid J. will not be able to come to us, and, indeed, on the 28th, we received a letter from him saying so, and telling us he had gone with his regiment, eighty miles by train, and then a three days' march under a burning Bengal sun.

Tuesday 31st. Face-ache again, which lasted exactly twenty-four hours. H. also has been unwell with a bad cold.

[*August*, 1855.]

Saturday, 4th. I have had a bad cold and cough, which pulled me down again just as I was getting better, however, I was allowed to take a drive in Mrs Grant's carriage, which I enjoyed very much.

Wednesday 8th. I have been ill again.

A telegraphic message says that Lieutenant Toulmin, of John's regiment, was killed. He led his four hundred men against ten thousand Sonthals across a nullah, they stuck in the mud and he, and a good many of his men, were killed.

Monday, 13th. John's name is in the paper as wounded, but it is not the case, as we have heard from him since the date specified. The loss of his left arm at the battle of Chillianwalla is quite enough to last him his life.

Wednesday, 15th. We set off at half-past three this morning, to go to the Hills for change. Our first stage was Bussee, about seventeen miles. One of the bullocks of our baggage cart died after an illness of two hours, from eating grass, and the owners, with long beards, cried like children.

Saturday, 18th. At Hurripoor, Mr. Blair* rode over from Sabathoo and breakfasted and dined with us; we all went out and H. caught some fish for dinner. H. saw three men burning a young woman who had died in the morning; these men were the three husbands of the woman, so they practise polyandry in this hill district.

Monday, 20th. Major Rose† had kindly asked us to breakfast, and spend our first day at Simla with him. I came from Kalka in a Janpan, a kind of chair carried by four men. We have given them each a suit of warm clothes, and they look very nice. We have a very comfortable little

*9th. Lancers.
†9th Lancers.

house for which we pay £10, but we shall not be able to stay a whole month. On a clear day we have a beautiful view of the snowy range. The scenery of the Himalayas is certainly very grand, but I was disappointed in its beauty, perhaps I expected too much.

Friday, 24th. We went to the theatre and saw first *Love in humble life,* the actors were bad; then, *Indiana and Charlemagne,* in French, which was very good. The third piece *The Merry Monarch,* we did not see, as I was too tired to stay for it. Between the plays, instead of a band, a man played on a very rattling piano.

Monday, 27th. Mr. Grant, who is here on leave, dined with us. I had the most acute face-ache for half an hour, it came on in the middle of dinner, and left me shivering and shaking all over, and with my teeth chattering from the excessive pain.

Thursday, 30th. We went yesterday morning early, to Maharsoo, one march in the interior, the road to it was very pretty. The scenery improves very much as you go more into the Hills.

[*September,* 1855.]

Friday, 7th. Very fine morning, but at 1 o'clock it began to rain,and we went to dine at Major Rose's in a regular downpour. We met there, Captain and Mrs. Montgomery, 13th B. N. I. they brought their two little girls, of three and two years old.

Saturday, 8th. We breakfasted at the Montgomerys and after luncheon started on our homeward journey. We brought away a little puppy, one of six, whose mother had been carried off by a leopard that morning. We reached

Umballah on Thursday morning 13th, and came to our new house, which is a great improvement on our old one.

Friday, 21st. We went to a Ball given by the 5th N. I. Regiment.

Satutday, 22nd. We gave a little dinner party to Capt. and Mrs. Mc Farlane; he has been given a troop in the 3rd Dragoon Guards.

Tuesday, 25th. We drove early in the morning to the city of Umballah, about three miles from Cantonments, where the civilians live, it is a very pretty drive. Bad face-ache all day. Henry went to Mess, a farewell dinner to Capt. Mc Farlane. They go to Calcutta, by river—float down in a boat from Meerut.

[*October*, 1855.]

Saturday, 6th. H. went to a Court-martial on an Artillery-man for attempted murder. He told a man, there was a bottle of spirits, hidden somewhere in a well, and while the man was looking about for it, tilted him in; however, he managed to keep himself up till the would-be murderer thought his victim was safe, and had gone away. He then called out for help, and after some time, he was pulled up a good deal exhausted. The Artillery-man was transported for fourteen years.

Wednesday, 17th. We have bought two little grey ponies for our carriage. I cut my hand to-day dreadfully, in two places with glass; none of the doors, of which the upper parts are of glass, have any handles; they stick from bad paint, and in trying to open one, my hand went quite through.

Monday, 22nd. Our carts set off yesterday, and we left this morning to go into the Jungle for a week's shooting.

Two tents, two carts, goat, Crib,* the puppy, little tame squirrel, and servants, H. on horseback, and I in the Bullock Gharie. We reached our tents at nine, and were glad to find our breakfast ready. During the heat of the day, I amused myself with my German books, and played two games of chess, both of which I won. In the cool of the evening, we took a walk, and the puppy followed us quite well, and at night, slept in our tent and kept guard, barking, when any one came near, though he is not two months old. H. has called him the "*Sogdolager*" (the name of a large trout found in American lakes.)

Tuesday, 23rd. We came to Jejardree and took advantage of the Dâk Bungalow, though I much prefer the tent. On the way we had a beautiful view of Jumnotree and Jungotree, the range of eternal snow, in which the Jumna and Ganges take their rise. At breakfast, after our little squirrel had finished his bread and milk, he jumped into H's hot cup of tea, which seemed to hurt him very much, but we dipped him in cold water, and in half an hour, he was perfectly well again. H. shot some snipe, which were very good.

Wednesday, 24th. We reached our tent at Chilkana (about 15 miles) at nine, and spent the day as usual. H. went out shooting at three, but only brought home two snipe and a quail, with three Shikaries to help him! I took a walk with the Ayah, and our two dogs; the goat insisted on making one of the party, and followed as well as the dogs.

Thursday, 25th. H. went out shooting in hopes of finding some deer, but he came back disappointed with only a few snipe. I went out in the gharie to the banks of a small but rapid river, and walked a long way, it was so enjoyable, perfectly cool although the sun had risen some time. After

*an Irish terrier we brought out from England.

luncheon, we sent off the carts, and we followed soon after, and encamped on the banks of the river Jumna. H. threw the puppy in to have his first swim, before he was two months old; he did not seem to mind; and afterwards H. took him to the other bank, then called him, and he swam across without the slightest hesitation, so he will be a good water dog. H. shot a fish in the water, which we eat for breakfast and it was delicious. In the morning we had a small tent pitched close to the river, and I had such a delightful bathe for the first time in a river. I forgot to take off my rings, and all of a sudden felt my wedding ring slipping from my finger; my diamond ring was gone! Fortunately the bed of the river was sandy, and after feeling about for a little while, I actually found it. Saturday evening we returned to the Dâk bungalow, and were caught in a dust storm. The air was so full of it that it became quite dark.

Monday, 29th. Went to Malana to our large tent, but the servants and small tent did not arrive until past two, and we did not get our first meal until half-past four, and in the meantime took a little Indian corn to allay the pangs of hunger.

Tuesday, 30th. We returned to Umballah. Our other Khidmutgar that we left behind was out, so we got no breakfast. H. went to Mess to breakfast, and brought me back a sandwich, so we were not as badly off as yesterday and had luncheon at two.

It was so cold in the tent last night, that in the morning, we found our little squirrel quite stiff and motionless, his eyes wide open, but quite insensible, and we thought dead However, H. put him against his warm neck, and in a short time, he actually recovered and was as well as ever.

Wednesday, 31st. Our ponies are broken into harness, so we took a drive, and called on Col. and Mrs Grant, and heard the glee singers; and Sergeant Bristow sang some capital comic songs.

[*November*, 1855.]

Thursday, 1st. The 10th Queen's Infantry arrived in the station this morning. We rode out to see their encampment, the officers dined at Mess; H. went. They march on Saturday.

Friday, 2nd. Their band played, but it was not a good one. The 81st that passed through while we were in the jungle, I hear, have a much superior one.

Tuesday, 6th. Band evening. We went to a dinner party at Colonel Grant's and heard the Ethiopian Serenaders, performed by our soldiers; it was very good, only too long. Sergeant Bristow sang some comic songs, and we did not get home till past twelve, very late for India.

Wednesday, 7th. There are field days now three times a week, as the inspection by the General is drawing near. I went to see it to-day, skirmishers were sent out with pistols, which were rather difficult to load on such restive horses as they have in India. We dined at Dr Grant's —fourteen in number.

Thursday, 8th. H. went out stag hunting. Major Pratt sent us a delicious jar of hill honey.

Friday, 9th. We went to a ball at the 60th Mess (B. N. I.) and enjoyed it very well.

Wednesday, 14th. We dined at Colonel Grant's to meet Brigadier and Mrs. Hallifax. Miss Hallifax is engaged to the Hon. Captain Curzon, A. D. C. to the Commander-in-

Chief. He is the fourth or fifth son of Lord Howe. She sings beautifully and he seems very fond of music.

Friday, 16th. A large ball to the whole station, given by the 9th Lancers. Colonel and Mrs. Grant do not go to balls, so I had to receive the ladies, and give the move at supper to Mrs. Hallifax, the grand lady. Champagne supper and everything seemed to go off well.

Monday, 19th. A sad accident happened here on Friday. A young officer of the 60th N. I. was riding on the Mall, his saddle, I believe, turned round, and he fell off on his head. He, however, walked home, and did not think much of it, but he soon became delirious, and died on Saturday. They say a blood vessel broke, but I hear his brain was either diseased, or had something very singular about it. A piece of it was sent to Calcutta to be examined, his head was so constructed that the slightest blow must have killed him; he was only eighteen, and his mother lives at Agra.

Tuesday, 20th. Major and Mrs. Montgomery, and their two little girls came to stay with us, and I drove Mrs. M. to the band in the pony carriage.

Wednesday, 21st. Dined at Colonel Nuthall's to meet the Brigadier and Mrs. Hallifax.

Thursday, 22nd. General Johnstone inspected the 9th Lancers. I drove out to see the Inspection.

Friday, 23rd. We went to a dinner party at Brigadier Hallifax', and had plenty of very good music.

Saturday, 24th. The Montgomerys left us this evening, the children were troublesome, being very much spoilt, as most children are in India.

Sunday, 25th. Service at 11 o'clock; more English-like.

Wednesday, 28th. The Commander-in-Chief entered Umballah this morning. The whole of the troops in the station were out in review order to meet him, and seventeen guns were fired as a salute.

Thursday, 29th. A Levée was held at the Commander-in-Chief's, and all officers ordered to attend. I thought a Levée was optional.

Friday, 30th. Poor Mrs. E's sister has lost her husband at Lahore; he committed suicide; he was greatly in debt His father had sent him a large sum of money—I think about £3,000—to pay his debts some time ago, but instead of doing so, he spent the money. He had just drawn a cheque on his father which was dishonoured. He leaves a widow and one child.

[*December*, 1855.]

Sunday, 2nd. Thanksgiving day for the fall of Sebastapol.

Monday, 3rd. A gentleman called without sending in his card, as is usual. I did not know who he was, till he told me he was my cousin, Hugh Hodgson, whom I had not seen for fourteen or fifteen years. He lunched with us, and intended starting to-morrow on his way to England, but we persuaded him to send on his tents, and stay till Wednesday. Very soon after, Colonel Grant rode up to say the Upton's* whom we had asked to stay with us, had arrived, and were at the Dâk Bungalow. H. went there while I got their rooms prepared, and in less than an hour they arrived, with a little baby, not five months old, born at sea. I had the big tent prepared for Hugh, as our house was now full. He left on Wednesday at mid-day in the Bullock Gharie, my horse was waiting for him nine miles on, and his own horse took him the third part—in all, thirty miles.

*Lt. Upton just joined the 9th Lancers.

Friday, 7th. We went to the theatre to hear the Ethiopian Serenaders. Our band played, it was as before too long. The price of the tickets was three rupees (six shillings) each.

Monday, 10th. Mr Upton and H. went to Mess, as the 60th Rifles passing through, dined there.

Wednesday, 12th. The Uptons went to their own house this evening after tea, it is quite close and seems a very nice little bungalow.

Thursday, 13th. English Mail. We heard that H's cousin, Colonel James Campbell, who has just sold out of the 87th (Royal Irish Fusiliers) is dead. Mrs Upton and I dined with Mrs Grant; all husbands at Mess.

Friday, 21st. A telegraphic message from Delhi from the Arnolds* came asking where her brother Hugh was; we answered, "marched to Meerut on the 5th," and told them to come to us.

Monday, 24th. After breakfast, in walked William and Fanny Arnold, and—Hugh! I could not get them to stay here, they were engaged to go to the Civil Lines at Old Umballah, whither we sent them in the Bullock Gharie, after I had been to see the two babies at the Dâk Bungalow. They shewed me a beautiful stereoscope of Eddie, the eldest, who has been left in England; little Florrie‡ of seventeen months, is cutting her back teeth, and looked very poorly.

Hugh stayed here, they telegraphed to him to join them at Delhi, and thinking he had not seen enough of his sister, he came back with them. In the evening, we went to Col Grant's, he had a Christmas tree for the school children (soldiers' children); almost all the children in the station were there, and a great number of grown-up people.

Christmas Day. To church in the morning. Fanny and

*William Delafield Arnold, fourth son of Dr Arnold, of Rugby, married to my cousin Fanny, daughter of General Hodgson.

‡afterwards married to Robert Vere O'Brien.

the young baby (Hugh)* came to spend the day here, and we sent them and (big) Hugh back to Umballah in the Bullock Gharie. We dined at Dr Grant's. We had three presents of cakes, and other things, from the bazaar people but the servants, I believe, eat up every thing except the cakes. We divided £1 between them as a Christmas present.

Wednesday, 26th. Hugh started for Meerut at nine o'clock; the Arnolds also were to leave for up-country this morning. I sent Mrs. Upton my horse to ride yesterday and to-day.

Thursday, 27th. All the Hallifaxes, seven in number, came here to be photographed, and lunched with us. The photographs were not very successful, H. thought, but they were very pleased†. In the evening, as we were driving on the Mall, we passed an elephant with three horrid looking Fakirs on it; they paint their faces, and cover their naked black bodies with wood ashes, but they are obliged to wear some covering in cantonments. By the side of the elephant was another dreadful looking creature in a Palkee, carried by bearers; the natives have the greatest respect for them.

Monday, 1st. A dinner was given, by subscription, to the boys of the Lawrence Asylum, (for the children of soldiers) they marched down from Kussowlie, and are to stay here about a week. They are a very uninteresting looking set of boys. After dinner, Punch and Judy was performed by one of the soldiers, and then there were all sorts of games, running in sacks, jumping, running backwards, etc. Mrs. Grant distributed prizes of books to those who did best.

We went to a ball at the 60th N. I. Mess to dance the New Year in.

*afterwards H. O. Arnold-Forster.
†Photography was then in its infancy.

John's exploits with the Sonthals, copied from *The Times of India.*

"Lieutenant Delamain with a small body of men has made great havoc among large masses of the rebels. On one occasion one thousand came down on him and his eighty Sepahis on one flank, and eight hundred on the other; with his own hand he slew eight of the leading men, and a half-fledged Sepahi at his side is said to have cut down eleven. In about fifteen minutes the mass was seen to sway from side to side, and in five minutes more, they had all bolted."

[*January*, 1856.]

New Year's Day. No Service in the Church and no Band.

Friday, 4th. Mrs Grant had the school children of the 9th Lancers to dine in the Compound. A number of ladies and gentlemen and children went to see them, and Punch and Judy, which was performed afterwards. We left at four o'clock to see the Artillery practice with live shells and rockets, so pretty, the latter rather dangerous and erratic in their course.

Tuesday, 8th. The Band played in the soldiers' gardens, and is to do so every Tuesday; carriages are not allowed inside, but there are garden seats to sit on.

Monday, 14th. Miss Hallifax's wedding day. We were invited, and accordingly went to the Church Bungalow at half-past eleven. Captain Curzon soon arrived and the bride was not late; she was dressed in a white watered silk up to the throat, laced behind, a plain skirt very long, and a plain net veil reaching to the ground behind and fastened by a wreath round her head, sleeves of blond, and a blond frill round her neck; she had two bridesmaids, Miss Lloyd and Miss James, dressed in white, with blue trimmings; she was exceedingly composed. The bride's little brother and sister of five and three, and also her nephew of two (Bagot) were present, and insisted on talking during the service. After the ceremony, we all proceeded in our own carriages to the Brigadier's house, when the bride received a telegraphic message of congratulation from a married sister, Mrs. Woodhouse. The Brigadier took me in to breakfast, we sat down about twenty in number, including Mrs. Burne and the clergyman's wife (Mrs. Ellis), also Mrs. Hallifax's other married daughter, Mrs. Bagot. There were three or four short speeches, and then the bride changed her dress, and was driven, not away out of the Station, but to a small house close by, where they were to stay a few days before they took their long journey to Darjeeling, about 800 miles off, where Capt. Curzon of the 52nd Queen's Infantry has an appointment—the charge of a Depôt of invalids.

The Bridegroom, as well as all the officers attending the wedding, was in full dress uniform.

Wednesday, 16th. We went to a very pleasant ball at the Artillery Mess, given by them and the Civil and Military Staff, to the 9th Lancers. The Brigadier danced the first quadrille with me, and took me into supper. While there, an officer told me he had heard from Captain Gott, who is in the station, that J's bed had caught fire, and his hand had been a good deal burnt, but that he was quite well again; he had been reading in bed, and fallen asleep; having only one arm, he must have found it difficult to help himself.

Thursday, 17th. The squirrel was let out into the garden to-day, against my orders, and did not come back in the evening, as he always used to do. I suspect he has made himself a nice place, in one of the trees, and thought he would like to be quite independent; we were very sorry for he was so exceedingly tame and playful; we have had him just three months and a half.

Saturday, 19th. There was a parade this morning, to which H. went, after a little while his horse came galloping back alone, which frightened me. I sent someone to see what was the matter, H. had been thrown by his horse putting his foot into a rat hole and falling down; he was not much hurt, only his foot was slightly strained.

We sent off a cart with our small tent, and went to a place a few miles off. H. has got leave for a month. The camels did not come in time, so we could not go a whole march. We have got an elephant, and Mr. Sarel has lent us his howdah. H. rode his brown Arab, and I went in the Gharie; we brought our two ponies, the two dogs, and a goat, four camels, and a bullock cart, and about twenty servants, three men to take care of the elephant, two for the camels, and one for the cart, so we muster pretty strong.

Sunday. We came on to Malana, and on Monday to Billaspoor. H. shot two large vampire bats, of which there are a great number, they have heads like a small dog, and their body is covered with hair, they have little claws at the extremity of their wings, by which they hang on to the branches of trees, and sleep during the day. A man came and asked for the bodies of these creatures to cure children with bad eyes! they use the blood I believe.

In the evening, we went to a kind of lake, about a mile off, and got a teal and some snipe.

On Tuesday, we came to Kidderabad, and pitched our large tent close to a pond. H. shot several times at some ducks on it, but did not succeed in killing any. The road is now very bad, as we are quite out in the jungle; sometimes we have to go up and down steep little hills, then across a river, deep and wide, in the rains, but now shallow enough to ford, with a quarter of a mile of stones on each side. Sometimes the track, (not road) takes us along the dry bed of a nullah, or mountain torrent, where there are huge stones, weighing several hundredweight; in such cases, and whenever the road is very bad, I get out of the Gharie and ride on one of the ponies, or on H's horse, if he is not using it. Often I have to go seven or eight miles, or even the whole march, on horseback.

Wednesday, 25th. We breakfasted before starting, as the servants were afraid to travel during the night, having heard that a tiger was lurking about the road, and had already eaten up a number of bullocks and their drivers. The sun is rather hot in the middle of the day, but a shawl on my hat, falling down over my back while riding, prevented my feeling it very much. We came to Kalesur, and encamped on the banks of the river Jumna. H. went on the elephant and brought in the first deer.

Thursday, 24th. H. set off on the elephant, and I rode the whole way on H's horse to Pauntee, through the jungle, there was scarcely a beaten track, and I lost my way. I had two servants with me, but they knew nothing of the road; we at length reached a village, the houses of which were built entirely of straw, both roof and walls, here we were able to enquire our road. I do not believe the inhabitants had ever seen a white person before, much less a lady, and on horseback too! We again pitched our tent near the river. H. bought a net, and caught a few fish, which were very good. On Friday we had some rain, and walking by the river, were caught in a heavy shower. We intend to remain for a few days at Pauntee.

Saturday, 26th. H. persuaded me to go out with him on the elephant for a day's shooting; at first the motion made me feel very sick, so he gave me a little brandy, which burnt my throat but cured me. We saw a good many deer, but to my great relief, H. did not kill any; he knocked over a porcupine, however, and the elephant was so frightened that he first began to stamp, and at last fairly ran away. We came to Nagpore in the evening.

Monday, 28th. I went out again on the elephant, and we had eight men to beat the jungle, when H. killed two deer, quite dead. Another elephant came this evening, so we sent the other away.

Tuesday, 29th. Came on to Jussawallah, seven miles, and had to cross the Jumna, the carts, camels, and men, etc. in a boat. H. and I were on the elephant, and a grass cutter came with us on foot; we crossed at a fordable place, but the current was so strong I was afraid the man would have been carried away; he seemed very much frightened, but caught hold of the elephant's tail, and we afterwards gave him a rope to hold on by; the water was up to his middle in the deepest part. About 8 o'clock it commenced to rain furiously, and soon the thunder burst over our heads, I think I never heard it so loud and near. The servants had our little tent, but the horses were out in the pelting rain, which continued all night, and until 12 o'clock the next day. After breakfast, H. had his beautiful horse brought inside the outer kernaut of the tent. Luncheon over, we took a walk, and I found my over-shoes very useful, as the water was everywhere an inch or two deep.

Thursday, 31st. After a cup of tea (which we always

have in India before getting up) we set off for Umbiwallah to breakfast, which we did not have till 2 o'clock. Afterwards we went on to Dehra, where the tent was not up, or dinner ready till 8 o'clock.

[*February*, 1856.]

Friday, 1st. We went to see Rajpore, at the foot of the Hills, about six miles from Dehra, where H. lived for six months when he was in India before, about seven or eight years ago. His house is entirely out of repair, no one having lived in it since; the roof of one of the rooms has entirely fallen in. The cantonment of Dehra is very pretty, everything looked green and pleasant; the houses, too, are much better than any I have seen, most of them having two stories.

Saturday, 2nd. We rode out in the evening by the side of a very narrow canal; at every twenty or thirty yards there is a fall of several feet. H. had the dogs put in, and the poor puppy was nearly drowned, the Syces had to go to his rescue.

Monday, 4th. We had a very heavy shower of rain yesterday. We came on to Lutchuwallah. H.. shot a very large cat, he thought it was a panther!

On Tuesday we came to Jumnotri,—a long march; lost our way and went over a dreadful road, mended with branches of trees; we ought not to have gone over it at all, and had to retrace our steps to get on to the right road again. We remained here, and on Wednesday H. brought home an immense deer (spotted). After H. comes back from shooting, I always take a walk with him down to the river, if we are near it, which is generally the case, and our dhobie (washerman) being fond of the water! brings the net to catch fish.

On Thursday we came on to Hurdwar, a beautiful native city, with a great many fine buildings; it is situated on the river Ganges. Numbers of people come to bathe in this river, as a religious ceremony. There is a fair held here every year, and a very grand one every seven years—the well known fair of Hurdwar, when thousands of people come from Thibet, Lahore and, in fact, from the most distant parts of India, and rush down at a particular time to a particular place, to bathe; the crowd is so great that numbers lose their lives.

Friday, 8th. We have now reached the furthest point to which we intend to go, and to-day set out on our return. A coolie brought us our letters this morning.

We reached Umballah on Monday, the 18th. In re-crossing the river Jumna, the loaded cart very nearly came to grief; there is a very steep descent to the river, the bullocks were taken out, and about twenty men (our servants) eased it down, but when it was just going on to the boat or raft, the rope slipped that held the boat, and the wheels got down between the boat and the shore, and though there was not space enough to let the wheels quite down, the cart had to be entirely unladen before it could be got right. The bullocks were driven into the water, and swam across beautifully, two of them however, returned, but were soon sent back again. The servants got us some very good eels, which H. liked very much, they were found under large stones, and killed with sticks, they were about a foot long.

At Malana (one march from Umballah) we found Captain Coare, who had been ill, and had got a month's leave; he dined with us. There has been a very gay wedding near here, amongst the natives of a high class, they were just going back to their respective homes. Some nautch girls, however, performed, which H. and Captain Coare went to see for a short time in the evening ; they kept it up all night. The performance consists in a kind of dance and monotonous singing.

H. has killed about fourteen deer altogether; a man came to him, and asked for the eyes of the deer to make medicine for his children !

The first thing we heard at Umballah was of the almost sudden death of Dr. Grant, of the 9th Lancers, from the bursting of a blood vessel in the chest, which suffocated him. His poor wife was the first person to find him dead, she is now at Colonel Grant's.

The gun never fires now on account of the illness of Mrs. Forsyth, whose house is situated close to the gun—they say if it were fired, she would die. She has just come out from England with her sister and two little girls, and has lately had twins (girls), but only one survives, and she is in a most precarious state.* Her husband, who is in the Civil service, has been sent for from up-country.

Friday, 29th. I rode out to see a Brigade Review, the 9th Lancers, the 4th Lancers (native), the Artillery, and two regiments of Native Infantry—the 5th and the 60th.

[*March*, 1856.]

Monday, 3rd. The gun fired again to-day. We are now able to keep true time ; when there was no gun to regulate it, every one went by his own watch, and many were late for church, etc.

Friday, 7th. H. sent the Sirdar (head bearer) to prison

*She eventually recovered.

yesterday, as we have lost so many things lately—a silver pen holder, three bladed knife, scissors, etc.—and yesterday, some pure silver was abstracted from the drawers. It could not be proved that he had stolen the things, so he was liberated.

I hear that an attempt has been made to burn down the house of Campbell, the milliner, etc. by shooting an arrow loaded with combustibles into the thatch; the arrow, fortunately, hit below and exploded on the wall, leaving a large mark. People suspect a rival milliner with having a hand in this atrocious design. The man was not caught.

Saturday, 8th. William Arnold walked into the room rather to my astonishment, as I believed him to be at Lahore; he is here on duty*. He lunched with us, but could not stay for dinner, as he is too busy.

Sunday, 9th. The weather is now very hot; it was not hotter than this in May last year; to-day the thermometer in the shade was 113°. Service has been altered from 11 to 7 o'clock in the morning; we went to church in the evening, and found the heat very oppressive.

Thursday, 15th. I dined at Mrs. Grant's, and met Mrs. Campbell, Mrs. Burne, and Mrs. Upton; all the husbands were at Mess, and at half-past nine they came in for music, and took their respective wives home. Mrs. Hutchinson is still staying with Mrs. Grant, she came about the end of November, her husband being with the force fighting against the Sonthals. Mrs. Grant never saw her before she went to stay there with her little baby. This is true Indian hospitality! Thermometer 85° in our cool house, and I hear other people had it at 92° indoors.

Thursday, 22nd. My brother John has become a captain by the death of an officer from cholera. He is thought

*He was Director of Public Instruction in the Punjaub.

very lucky to be a captain after only ten years' service. I hear Mr. Hutchinson has arrived, and they are both going to stay at Colonel Grant's sometime longer.

Monday, 26th. Inspection. I rode out to see it. General Johnstone* inspected the regiment. A Sikh regiment has come to remain in the Station.

Tuesday, 27th. Foot (dismounted) Inspection at six in the evening. H. drove me there. Inspection dinner.

Thursday, 29th. H. did not dine at Mess again though it is his usual night for doing so. We went to the theatre and saw *The Rivals* acted by amateurs. Mr. Chalmers was Capt Absolute, he is the grandson of Mrs. Bishop, of Exeter. I enjoyed it very much, though some of the officers did not act well, Mrs. Malaprop being decidedly bad. It was great fun to see the ladies walk, and naturally they talked with very gruff voices. The tickets for admission were four rupees for single, and six rupees (12 shillings) for double tickets. Colonel and Mrs. Grant went away to stay with Mrs. Grant's sister, Mrs. Shakespeare, who has just come out from England.

Friday, 30th. H. read in the papers that a surgeon is to be tried for manslaughter. A Capt. Jameson, at a Dâk Bungalow somewhere near Calcutta, being in pain, wrote to the doctor and requested him to send two grains of morphia to procure sleep. The doctor made up a pill of ten grains, the officer took it, and of course never woke again.

[*April,* 1856.]

Thursday, 3rd. The band practises in a little house near our garden, I generally walk out in the morning and listen to it, it is considered a very good one; Colonel Grant

*Lt-Colonel Montagu Cholmeley Johnstone.

being a musican himself takes a great interest in it. We dined with Mr* and Mrs Campbell, he is a civilian, and gets some thousand rupees a month; she sings very well, and we sang some duets together.

Saturday, 5th. Colonel Grant returned this morning, leaving Mrs. Grant to stay a little longer with her sister.

Sunday, 6th. Went to Church in the morning, it was very pleasant and cool there, but about 10 o'clock it blew hard, and soon the whole air was full of dust, so that you could not see the sky or any distance before you. Of course we had all the doors and windows shut immediately, but nothing could keep the terrible dust out, and in an uncarpeted room footsteps made marks exactly like those after a fall of snow. After five o'clock, although the wind was just as high, there was no dust in the air!

Monday, 7th. H. drove me out in the evening, and I set him down at the Mess to read the papers before dinner, driving myself home. I then had a chair brought out into the verandah, as usual, to sit there till dinner. Just at a quarter past seven, I felt my chair sway to and fro under me, and the whole house appeared to do the same. I knew, instantly, that it was an earthquake, it certainly was an awful feeling and I felt a little frightened. It had been very hot and a disagreeable kind of day.

Saturday, 12th. A full dress parade at 6 this morning to read to the soldiers of the station the appointment of Lord Canning, as Governor General of India. A salute of nineteen guns was fired.

H. has got six months' leave to go to the hills; we sent off our carts early on Thursday the 17th, and started ourselves at five, going the first few miles in our carriage, the rest of the way, H. rode, and I went in my janpan. The

*Afterwards Sir George Campbell.

road is very bad, at least half a foot deep in sand and dust which effectually concealed the numerous and deep ruts, so we were not sorry to leave the carriage, which could only go very slowly. We reached the Dâk Bungalow at half-past ten, and found that the carts had not arrived, nor did they till one o'clock ; they came by another and worse road and were twelve hours going seventeen miles. We had expected a nice supper, and our beds to be ready for us. I had fortunately put a candle and candle-stick into my janpan, so we were not without light amongst other wants and there was a beautiful moon.

Friday, 18th. This is a very small and hot Bungalow, thermometer at 11 a.m. 95°, at 3 p.m. 98°. The tatties are broken and useless, there is, however, a punkah.

We were very glad to leave Bussee at half past-six in the evening. H. went in a dhooly instead of riding, we had a few drops of rain and some thunder and lightning. We reached the hotel (so called) at Kalka at noon on Saturday. Our own servants provided breakfast, and then left for Kussowlie ; we managed to get a grilled chicken and some bread from the Hotel people for lunch, and set off at four, reaching Kussowlie in time for dinner.

We have fifty-eight coolies, and some mates to look after them and our effects. Our few things will cost upwards of £6 for carrying them forty miles ; we paid under £1 for bringing them the same distance in the plains (in carts.)

The new road to Simla is soon to be opened, and trucks used for luggage. We passed a poor cow that had fallen from the hill on to the path, it is wonderful that they do not oftener miss their footing, as they have to traverse such steep places in search of food.

Sunday, 20th. We were at Hurripoor which we found very

hot, the thermometer 80°, while at Kussowlie it was only a little over 70°. We reached Siree at six on Monday.

Tuesday, 22nd. We rose very early, had some cocoa, toast, and eggs, and started at six for Simla where we arrived at half-past nine, and went straight to a house, which we can hire by the day until we find one to suit us.

Wednesday, 23rd. We took a walk in the morning, and a ride in the evening, we like the house well enough, but the road up to it is so steep, narrow and dangerous, that we are obliged to walk up and down the hill, and mount and dismount our horses at the bottom, so we cannot possibly remain here. It is very difficult to get a house for less than the season, and as our stay is very uncertain, we do not like to tie ourselves down. At last, we found one which we could have by paying seventeen rupees a month extra, and taking it for two months certain. It is small, but will be large enough for us, and it is in a good central position close to the Mall; we came into it on Friday, 25th. H. dined at the Club of which he is an honorary member.

[*May*, 1856.]

Thursday, 1st. I was pleased and surprised this morning at hearing the note of the cuckoo. We had a terrible storm of thunder and lightning, with hail stones as big as marbles.

Sunday, 4th. We went to Church in the morning. It is quite delightful being in a real church again after the old barn at Umballah. The morning was quite fine and I did not see a cloud, but before even the prayers were over, a tremendous storm came on, the thunder made an awful accompaniment to the organ; as it became worse, the roar of the thunder hardly ceased for a second, and such vivid flashes of lightning followed each other in quick succession, while enormous hailstones rattled on the roof, almost drowning Mr Mayne's voice, and at last it became so dark that he could hardly see to read his sermon. I could not help wondering whether there was a lightning conductor, for if the spire had been struck, it would have been a serious matter. On coming out, I had to walk through the clouds to my janpan, which was quite wet, not being made to resist such rain. The storm ceased about two o'clock, and in the evening we took a long walk.

Tuesday, 6th. We went to a picnic at the Waterfalls, by invitation of Lord William Hay.

Thursday, 8th. Mr Mayne* has service in the church every morning at seven. At noon we went to Gutoj, six miles off, to call on Major and Mrs. Bagot, he commands a Goorkha regiment there; we found three officers of our regiment also paying a visit. Major and Mrs. Bagot made us all stay to luncheon, which was at three o'clock, and was their dinner. There were two Irish gentlemen, called Hutchinson (brothers), staying there, so we were quite a party; they had come to visit India, and were very anxious to see "the rains." We spent a very pleasant afternoon, and returned to Simla by eight in the evening.

Friday, 9th. I was somewhat the worse for being out so much in the middle of the day, the sun has great power. I had severe pains in my head and dizziness. I fancy it was a slight sunstroke.

Monday, 12th. We started at eight o'clock for Mahasoo to a picnic given by Lord William Hay. I was there introduced to a Sardinian Duke, the Duke of Vallombrosa, who is staying at Simla; he is a young man who has travelled

*Rev. F. Otway Mayne.

much, and was at the taking of Sebastopol as an amateur. After breakfast, we went down the hill a couple of miles to see a grand fair; several thousand people were assembled, and a native Rajah who had come down on an elephant; he gave us some flowers and put some scent on our handkerchiefs. The principal amusement was a kind of swing or whirligig very much like those at an English fair, of which there were twelve or fourteen in constant motion. Then, first some men began shooting with bows and blunt arrows, the target being a man only a few yards off with his back towards the shooter, he kept in continual motion to prevent the arrow from touching him, and was generally successful in his endeavours, but great was the shouting and jumping about, if the arrow hit the moving target. Next came three Nautch girls who sang and at the same time stamped their feet to make the numerous bells and ornaments on their ankles tinkle, then they would put themselves into attitudes or throw themselves on the ground singing the same words and air over so many times that one got quite sleepy and tired of it; lastly eight men and one old woman came forward and performed a kind of dance, very slowly, with their arms extended, moving their hands about and looking very much as if they were wringing their hands in pain and grief, they reminded me of the figures that go round on a street organ. We found it very hot down in this valley, and were thankful for some claret cup, which Lord William had provided. I, however, wore a hat instead of a bonnet* which prevented my feeling the sun so much. When we reached Lord William's house at Maharsoo, we found a nice tiffin laid out in the room we had breakfasted in and we returned to Simla before dark, after a very pleasant day. H. took two photographs, but they were not successful.

*Hats were not much worn in those days.

Friday, 16th. The Duke called here, he is going shortly to Kashmīr. In the afternoon we had another fearful storm. I watched the forked lightning from the window, and never saw it so vivid and strong, one clap of thunder burst immediately over our house and shook it all over, the ūsual large hailstones accompanied it, verily the Hills is the place to witness a fine storm! I have a bad cold, and pain in the nerves of my head. I was weighed to-day, and find I am only 7st. 8lbs., while in England I weighed 9st. 2lb.!

Friday, 23rd. I chaperoned Miss Baker to a ball given by the members of the Simla Club, of which H. is one, there were about an equal number of ladies and gentlemen; the club rooms are small so the quadrilles were very crowded; we left at 2 a.m.

Saturday, 24th. We started off to go a few marches into the interior of the Hills; we rode to Mahasoo and instead of the Dâk bungalow we went to the house of a Captain Hay, who is in the plains, and wants to sell his house. We went part way on the new road; our dogs ran after a pariah dog, which so frightened the horses that H's. nearly threw itself down with fright; it was very dangerous, as the new road has no railing, is not very wide and has a frightful precipice at the side.

Sunday, 25th. We found plenty of books, sermons, etc., and at eleven left for Fargoo; we walked a great part of the way as it was mostly down hill. It was only three miles, and when we reached the bungalow it looked so uninviting, that we went on after luncheon to the next, about five or six miles further. I went part of the way in my Dandy, which is merely a long, strong pole, with a carpet tied to it, forming a very comfortable seat; it is carried by two men at a time.

Monday, 26th. I cannot say much for the bungalow here (Theog) but it has a pretty view, and is on a high hill.. We came on to Muttiana, mostly on the new road; in some places a kind of terrace is built outside the rock, with logs of wood, a tremendous precipice beneath, and over-hanging cliffs above; at one place H's horse put its foot through up to the fetlock, and we were obliged to be constantly on the look out for holes where the soil covering the planks had been partially washed away; our march was twelve or fourteen miles. We found Mr. Grant* here in tents, ill with fever and ague, so he could not come to dine with us. We took a long walk of five miles in the evening.

Tuesday, 27th. After a cup of tea and a biscuit we started, and instead of going by the new road round the hill, we resolved to go over it, thereby saving some six or seven miles, and the scenery well repaid us. For the first two or three miles the road was good, with a constant, though gentle ascent; when we came to the top of the hill a strong wind blew the clouds right in our faces, and the cold was intense. In a short time we had heavy rain and cloud mixed, with thunder and lightning besides, and to make matters worse, the road was now so bad that we were obliged to dismount. My horse had tried to take me up almost a perpendicular place, and in struggling, nearly fell, and actually put its hind feet down the Khud, fortunately not a very frightful one, but it was with the greatest difficulty that the Syce who was leading it managed to pull it up, I now thought it prudent to dismount. After this we had regularly to climb up rocks, and the horses did it beautifully, though H's was nearly down once on a large stone or rock, six or seven feet square, where it could find no hold for its feet and the rain had made the stone

*Mr. Frank Grant, 9th Lancers, nephew of Colonel Hope Grant, and son of Sir Francis Grant, R. A.

very slippery. When we had passed the worst part we got on our horses again, but soon had to dismount, and walk about five or six miles, most of the way down hill, the path was soaking wet and so slippery, I could scarcely keep my feet, though in some places it would have been most dangerous to slip. H. had an umbrella, but I preferred pinning a shawl over my hat which kept me dry as far as my waist, my habit was in a fearful state of mud. After about an hour it cleared up, and I was not sorry to be able to ride again after my long walk, the road we came over is a "pucka-dundee"—a mountain foot path. When we reached the Dâk Bungalow, we had a fire lighted and I dried what I could of my garments, but our luggage was all behind except the provisions with the cook, whom we had sent on before. We got a good breakfast at twelve o'clock, but it was past one before I could change my clothes. Mr. Grant had intended coming with us, but he was too ill in the morning to leave his bed, and it was really fortunate, under the circumstances, that he did not attempt it.

Wednesday, 28th. Mr Grant arrived early this morning, and just before we all sat down to breakfast a great storm came on, so he only just escaped a wetting. He spent the day with us, but was not strong enough to accompany us in our walk, when H. shot a pheasant.

Thursday, 29th. Mr Grant left for Kashmir—about seventy three marches, he is going to send the pony back (which belongs to Colonel Grant) when he is strong enough to walk, for no pony can travel where he is going.

We intend staying at this place, Narkunda, for several days. We went up a hill called Whatoo, about six miles off, and when we reached the top we saw a storm coming on. We found an old roofless house, where we hoped the walls might give us a little shelter; the horses were taken in, and the thunder and lightning began. This house was quite on the top of a hill, 10,000 feet above the level of the sea. We protected ourselves pretty well with the help of an umbrella, and eat our luncheon, after which, H. said it was too cold to stay, and we should find more shelter down the hill. So off we set in the middle of the storm, the wind nearly blew me away; in a few minutes, I was wet through, and as we had to descend a steep hill on wet grass, I nearly slipped down at every step I took, and the only approach to shelter we could find, was under trees, which I thought too dangerous in a storm. At last, the coolies discovered a place, but we had to go up a very steep hill, and then found ourselves under a projecting rock, which afforded a very good shelter. The men soon got some sticks together which H. lit with his gun, and we had a nice little fire before which I dried my things as well as I could. It cleared up in less than half an hour, and then we went to the top of the hill again, and I took a little sketch of the roofless house which had been our first shelter, and where we ought to have remained until the storm was over. We walked most of the way back, as it was down hill, and I went to bed, very tired, soon after dinner.

Friday, 30th. Mr. Henderson of the 32nd Queen's Infantry breakfasted with us. Three Germans also came to the Bungalow, Hermann, Adolph and Robert.* They are travelling for scientific purposes, (magnetic surveys in the Himalayas), and are going on to Kashmir. They have three or four hundred coolies to carry their things.

We left Narkunda at two, on our way back to Simla, and took care to come by the new road, but it turned and twisted about so much that I thought we should never

*One of these brothers—I think Robert—was murdered sometime after in the Hills.

reach Mattiana; it must be about eighteen miles by this route.

Saturday, 31st. We had a terrific storm during the night. We left directly after breakfast, and at Theog, half way, halted, and took luncheon under a shed; we then came on to Fargo, about eighteen miles altogether, the Bungalow looked quite inviting and actually had a carpet which none of the others possess on this line.

[*June*, 1856.]

Sunday, 1st. We halted here (Fargo). H. proposed going down the Khud to the river, which he said was only about three miles off. We had the horses led, and we walked down a very steep hill covered with large stones; when we had gone six miles we found we had much further to go, but, as we had come so far, we determined to persevere, and at last reached the river, about ten miles off, having walked the greater part of the way. It was very pretty when we got down to it, but the sun was very hot. We had brought luncheon with us, and rested, we thought, for a couple of hours (H's watch had got out of order); we then set out on our return, but soon found by the sun that it must be about six o'clock. I had ordered my Dandy to come, and we met it when we had gone about one third of the way, and by the time we were half way back it was perfectly dark, with no moon. We then rested in a village, and at last procured a strong pole, and with a rope tied a horse cloth to it and so made a Dandy for H. and after a great deal of trouble got five men for it. I had four men for my Dandy—only two carry it at one time placing the pole on their shoulders, with a thick pad underneath, and they constantly change shoulders to ease themselves. We had a great row, however, for one of the

Syces* went into the village to make the men come, and they said he had beaten one of the boys, and made such a noise about it that I was rather afraid they would take revenge on us, but at last we started; the Syces led the horses very carefully up the bad road, full of ravines, rocks, and stones. I took a long neck ribbon and tied it to Crib's collar to prevent his being taken away by a panther or leopard, but was obliged to let the puppy take its chance and we all reached the Bungalow safely at 9 o'clock. Sometimes I was carried with my feet hanging over a frightful precipice, when a false step of either of my two men would have sent me down below. I must have walked altogether about twelve miles, and did not feel very tired. We found English letters which had been sent out from Simla.

Monday, 2nd. We came to Simla, twelve miles, walking down all the hills. In the evening, all the sinews of every part of my body ached, and were so painful that I could scarcely move about the room. It is caused by the unusual exertion of walking so many miles down hill, and my feet are covered with blisters from the stones.

Saturday, 9th. Colonel and Mrs. Hope Grant arrived at Simla. Wednesday was a pouring day. Certainly this must be "the rains."

Friday, 13th. A second ball given by the members of the Club, we did not go though H. subscribed to it. It is in celebration of the Peace. †

Saturday, 21st. H. has been suffering from lumbago and rheumatism, the effects of the rain and damp. We therefore decided on throwing up our leave and returning to Umballah. We set off to-day and reached Kussowlie in two marches. H. dined at Mess, and I with Mr. and Mrs. Campbell, and spent a very pleasant evening.

*Horsekeeper.
† After the Crimean War.

We reached Umballah at seven a.m of the 25th, travelling from Kalka during the night in two dhoolies. Puppy ran the whole way from Kussowlie, about forty-five miles, and was not very tired.

Monday, 20th. The rains appear to have stopped, and those which fell at Simla must have been what are called, the Chota Bursat, or little rains. The air is very hot, but the grass is beautifully green, very different from the burnt up plains we left just two months ago.

[*July*, 1856.]

Tuesday, 1st. I rode on H's horse to the muster. Poor Crib was taken ill with giddiness, he snarled and growled when touched.

Thursday, 3rd. It rained nearly all day. The Duke of Vallambrosa called, and H. met him again at Mess, directly after which he proceeded to Calcutta.

Sunday, 20th. Went to Divine service at the Artillery barracks. One of the Chaplains is on leave of absence, so we only have morning service every other Sunday in our "barn". Thanksgiving for the Peace.

Saturday, 26th. Crib and puppy killed an enormous rat called a Bandicoot. Later on H. went down a kind of well he has had made for keeping meat in, when he saw a pair of eyes glaring at him out of the dark, he put the dogs down and they had a great fight with, and eventually killed, an enormous wild cat.

We have only had rain on nine days this month.

[*August*, 1856.]

Friday, 1st. We drank tea at Colonel Grant's, met a pleasant little party and had some good music. A large bat flew into the room, and soon settled on my bare neck. I remained quite still until it was taken off, when it bit most furiously anything within its reach. There is a report that the 9th Lancers are to be sent to Meerut this cold weather. I believe it is a very pleasant Station.

Wednesday, 6th. Mr. Franklyn, our new doctor, arrived yesterday, and breakfasted with us this morning, he was formerly in the 3rd Light Dragoons.

Friday, 8th. H. went round the guards, being Field Officer of the week. Our poor dog Crib has been very ill for several days. H. poured egg beaten up with wine down his throat, but nothing could save him, he would suddenly rush about in pursuit of an imaginary rat, or mouse, and then stagger and fall, he had several fits the day he died.

On opening a drawer to-day, I found, to my horror, two dresses bitten into shreds by a rat and quite destroyed.

Thursday, 28th. Mr. Gifford, a brother of the one we knew in the 3rd Light Dragoons, joined to-day, he came out to Calcutta in the same ship as Georgina and her husband, who have gone on to Singapore.

We have had a great deal of rain this month, only seven entirely fine days.

[*September*, 1856.]

Wednesday, 3rd. We had a small regimental dinner, Colonel and Mrs. Grant, Major Pratt and Dr. Franklyn.

Thursday, 4th. Three young squirrels fell out of their

nest, the Kidmutgar brought in two, the other had broken its leg, so he left it and the mother came and took it away. We put the two into a cage and placed it on a niche in the wall; the mother contrived to get one out of the cage and took it away, she then came back, pulled the cage to the ground in her endeavours to get the other out, and after eight or nine hours, I found the remaining one gone. She had managed it in some way, though the bars were so close it seemed impossible. After so much perseverance she deserved to succeed.

Friday, 5th. The cholera has come to the Station at last, three Artillery men went into hospital with it and died. At Lahore it has been awful, thirty men out of a hundred European Artillery have succumbed, and it is still raging there.

Monday, 8th. A fine west wind and the cholera has abated, very few men have died and those all Artillerymen

Thursday, 11th. H. is in command of the Regiment, as Colonel Grant is acting Brigadier while Colonel Hallifax is at Simla.

Thursday, 25th. Mr. and Mrs. Upton (of the 9th) and their two babies, left this evening for the Hills. I lent Mrs. Upton my dhoolie. Mrs. Grant has also gone again to Simla. A letter from Francisca told us of a soldier on his death-bed in the Crimea, having confessed to stealing two pheasants, off the lawn of the clergyman of Mentmore*—I happened to be there at the time these pheasants were stolen.

Monday, 29th. H. tried the experiment of killing a large hyena by strychnine; it belonged to an officer of the Regiment who had it when quite young, it is now full sized and has become vicious. A number of officers assem-

*The Rev. John Ouvry-North.

bled in Dr. Clifford's Bungalow and they forced 10 grains, sewn up in a piece of meat, down its throat, in ten minutes the poison began to take effect, and in a quarter of an hour it was dead.

Tuesday, 30th. Mr. Ellis called to take leave, he goes to Calcutta to pass in the languages, and to await the arrival of the Carabineers, into which Regiment he has exchanged. In the meantime he has to live on English pay—about one quarter of Indian pay—until the Regiment reaches Calcutta.

[*October*, 1856.]

Thursday, 2nd. Colonel Grant has gone to the Hills again.

Saturday 4th. Colonel Yule* called, he goes to Calcutta to-morrow, and then to get horses for the Regiment and will be away all the cold weather. We heard that Dr. Macleod, the Superintending Surgeon, Sirhind Division, died yesterday at Simla. H. is appointed President of the Committee of Adjustment which is a very disagreeable duty.

Tuesday, 7th. I rode out to see the horses leap.

I lost the middle diamond out of my ring yesterday, it was found to-day on the step of the verandah, sparkling in the sunshine.

Sunday, 12th. Went to church in the morning at six o'clock.

Wednesday, 22nd. We had a dinner party, Brigadier Hallifax, Mr.† and Mrs. Campbell, Colonel Riddell (60th. B.N.I.), Major Cobbe (87th Regiment), Capt. Frank Turner, (Bengal Artillery), Mrs. Hallifax is still in the Hills, and Mrs. Turner was not well enough to come.

*A Captain in the 9th and Brevet Lt. Colonel.
†Afterwards Sir George Campbell.

Friday, 24th. Capt. and Mrs. Robertson (8th Regiment), arrived early this morning to stay with us. He was obliged to go off to Delhi directly after breakfast; they have a nice little boy Charlie, thirteen months old.

I have written to my mother telling her I shall probably come home for a change in the spring of next year, on account of my health, which has been bad for a long time, and my brother John has promised to go with me. I have a very bad cough.

[*November*, 1856.]

The 32nd Regiment have begun their march from Kussowlie to Cawnpore. On the first day's march they were attacked with cholera and lost six men. They passed outside the station, not being allowed to enter Cantonments.

The Arnolds are staying with us, they sleep in their own tents which are pitched in the compound, they have two children and an English nurse (Roland), with them. H. photographed Flory a beautiful child of some two years, and Hugh Oakely is a very fine boy, of fourteen months, the eldest boy, Edward, has been left in England.

Thursday, 23rd. Inspection foot drill this afternoon, full dress, new uniform. The weather is very cold and we have begun fires in the evening.

Sunday, 23rd. Service at eleven now instead of early in the morning.

Monday, 24th. We drove out and saw the encampment of the two European Regiments, the 1st and 2nd Fusiliers. We all went to see the new church, I had never been inside it before, it appears to be nearly finished.

Friday, 28th. Mr. Sarel* of our Regiment and Mr. Chalmers of the Commissariat Department, gave a grand ball this evening, I was not well enough to go.

[*December*, 1856.]

Monday, 1st. Grand ball given by the Regiment. Though better, I was not strong enough to go to it, which was rather a disappointment, and I was kept awake half the night by the music. We have begun burning fires now all day long.

Monday, 8th. Hearing that Mr. Bell-Martin had arrived in the station to join the 9th Lancers, we went to the Dâk Bungalow, and made him and his wife come to us, she is very young, barely seventeen.

Thursday, 11th. Before the Martins arrived, H. had obtained ten days' leave to go into the jungle, we started after luncheon, leaving them in possession of our house until they can get their own ready. We went ten miles on the road to Sirhind. I had over-fatigued myself during the day, and was very ill in the night. I do not remember ever being so ill before, it ended in an hysterical fit, and violent shivering.

Friday, 12th. A troop of native Lancers encamped close to us this morning, there were about fifty of them, and they had no European officer with them. We did not march till after dinner when we went on ten miles; we found no tents up so we sat down in the open air and had some excellent coffee from concentrated essence, and bread and butter.

Saturday, 13th. A halt, very acceptable to me. H. went out into the jungle on his horse with two shikaries (hunters)

* Afterwards Govenor of Guernsey.

and two of our own men, he shot a fine nyl ghau (blue bull) the only one he saw; he pressed a cart into his service to bring it the few miles to our camp. The man came very unwillingly though he was to receive more than he could earn in two or three days at his regular work. The jackals came all round the tents at night making such a noise, and we hired an extra watchman to prevent the carcase from being eaten up by them and the jungle dogs.

Sunday, 14th. We came a very short march to Jellawara, about five miles. The country is perfectly flat for hundreds of miles; the only thing which breaks the perfect plain is the raised macadamized road which runs through it, and, with the electric telegraph wires has, at a little distance, the appearance of a railroad.

Monday, 15th. Came to Sirhind and encamped at a short distance from an old palace, mostly in ruins; there were two enormous stone wells, it was quite frightful to look down them, they were so deep. We are told that this is a dreadful place for thieves, and we had three watchmen from the village, though I think with a dog, two guns and a revolver, there was not much danger of our being molested.

Tuesday, 15th. We halted, and H. photographed all day and got some tolerably good pictures. There is an old burial ground here.

Wednesday, 17th. H. went round into the jungle to shoot. I came along the road back to Jellawara, and was glad to find the Persian wheel at rest; it was creaking the whole time we were here before. The water is brought up from the well by means of gurrahs tied to a very thick rope or ropes turned by a wheel to which two oxen are attached. H. went out again to *shikar* after dinner and saw some curious animals which he said looked something like camels.

Thursday, 18th. Came on to Oghana.

Friday, 19th. A large detachment arrived here during the night, and encamped not far from us. There were many officers and their wives, also soldiers belonging to different regiments proceeding from Landour to join their respective regiments. We made a march and H. brought in his beautiful horse dead lame, he fancies it must have put its foot in a hole. H. had to walk many miles.

Saturday, 20th. Had to leave the horse behind, and we came on into Cantonments, I had written to ask my cousins Mr. and Mrs. Charles Saunders, C. S.* to stay with us on their way up country, but had received no answer; the servants told us two ladies and a little child came here last night, and had gone to Colonel Grant. I soon found it was Miss Cautley† and Eddie Arnold, with his governess Miss Parsons, they had come out from England with the Saunders, who remained at Delhi. William Arnold sent us a telegraphic message to ask where his boy was.

Wednesday, 24th. We heard this evening that Mr. Sarel, who is out shooting, has met with an accident. Mr. Sinclair Smith, the assistant surgeon, went out to him by dhooly dâk, it appears that some part of his gun broke, which caused it to go off suddenly.

Friday, 25th. Christmas Day. To church in the morning, took the Bell-Martins and went to see the soldiers eat their dinner, after which there were speeches made. We went to a family dinner party at Brigadier Hallifax' and spent a pleasant evening. Major and Mrs. Bagot are now staying there as his regiment, the Nussurie Battalion, is to remain here for the winter months.

Saturday, 27th. H. bought a little white pony (Crab) at a sale.

*He afterwards had charge of the King of Delhi.
†Afterwards Mrs. Olpherts.

Sunday, 28th. H's horse came in from the jungle very lame. Mrs. Bell-Martin went to church with me in our bullock gharie and H. on his pony.

[*January*, 1857.]

(How little we all knew what this year was to bring forth!)

Thursday, 1st. A great deal of rain fell in the night, and several showers to-day. We dined at Mr. Franklyn's and met the Bell-Martins.

Friday, 2nd. We went to a ball given by the Station to the 60th. N. I. It was held in our Mess house, and was a very pleasant party.

Sunday, 4th. Service, for the first time, in our new church—St. Paul's. The Bishop of Madras arrived on Thursday, and consecrated it this morning, he preached a very good sermon, after which there was a collection made in order to finish the most important parts, and the Holy Communion was administered, for which I stayed. The service began at eleven, but was not over until past two. The afternoon service was at half past three, after which the Bishop held a confirmation. The new church is a beautiful building, capable of containing a thousand persons, it has been a very long time in building, and indeed is still very far from being finished, the flooring is not all laid down, and there is not one window completely glazed; some are partly filled with stained glass, and the rest are furnished with different coloured calicoes (I believe waxed) and it really looks very nice and neat. However unfinished, it is a delightful change from the "old barn" which has been used for the last fourteen years, ever since this has been a Station, I believe.

Friday, 9th. All the troops in the Station were out at a Brigade field day: 9th Lancers, two troops of Artillery, 4th Lancers (native), 1st and 2nd European Fusiliers, 5th and 60th Native Infantry, and Major Bagot's Goorkha Regiment. In the afternoon, at half past three, I drove Mrs. Bell-Martin to see the Artillery Practice.

Sunday, 11th. Sorry to find we had to go back to the old barn again, as the new church is too cold and damp.

Wednesday, 14th. H. goes very often to practise rifle shooting at long ranges, from 1, to 2,000 yards. Mr. Sarel went out to-day to see it in our bullock gharie, his hand is going on well, but it will be a long time before he can use it (he shot his thumb off while on a shooting expedition.)

Friday, 16th. I rode out on the little pony, and saw the Artillery Practice; we found it intensely cold. We went to a dinner party at Colonel Hope Grant's.

Saturday, 17th. Went to hear the band play, and walked about in the soldiers' gardens.

Wednesday, 21st. A dinner party at home. The Brigadier and Mrs. Hallifax, Mr. and Mrs. Campbell* Capt. and Mrs. Howard 4th. Lancers (native), and Miss Lloyd, Capt. Hutchinson, Mr. Franklyn and Mr. Gifford (9th Lancers). Last night, some animal—I suppose a wolf—came into the compound and devoured one of our kids.

Monday, 26th. It blew a hurricane all the morning with tremendous rain at intervals, and heavy rain in the afternoon. We drove out in the evening and it reminded me of the rainy season except in being much colder. We get well supplied with snipe by the officers who are on leave for a shooting expedition, and Mr. Head sent us in a nice wild duck.

*Afterwards Sir George Campbell, Lt. Gov. of Bengal.

Thursday, 29th. H. was on a Committee to-day to pick out thirty of the best horses from the 4th Cavalry (native) to be sent immediately to Meerut for the Carabineers. He went at eight, and did not return till past twelve to breakfast.

[*February*, 1857.]

Sunday, 1st. Went to church in our gharie and sent the buggy for the Bell-Martin's use. I went again in the afternoon with Mrs. B-M.

Monday, 2nd. A very rainy morning, the muster was dismissed.

Tuesday, 3rd. We were awakened in the night by a tremendous storm of thunder and lightning, with pouring rain; a very wet stormy day.

Wednesday, 4th. We went to a musical party at Mr. and Mrs. George Campbell's; she was the principal singer and has a beautiful voice; we were not at home till nearly two o'clock, very late for India.

Thursday, 5th. H. went to Mess. I was taken very unwell in the evening, with violent shivering, faintness, etc.

Friday, 6th. Slept very little, and got up with a bad head-ache, and feeling perfectly ill. Unfortunately we had a dinner party, Mr. and Mrs. Upton, Mr. and Mrs. Bell-Martin, Colonel Yule, Messrs. Sarel, Wilkinson, Hamilton, Blair and Dr. Sinclair Smith—all 9th Lancers Officers.

Saturday, 7th. Got up late. I was engaged to spend the day with the Trittons, and I went, but my head ached all the time, except when driving out with Mrs. Tritton. H. came at three to dinner, and we returned home to tea. Dr. Tritton told me he knew my father and mother, and my eldest brother died in his arms, at the age of ten months.

On Sunday when I woke, I found a rash had come out all over me, large red spots with a long blister in the middle, I believe chicken pox; I kept indoors till Saturday. Mrs. Upton allowed her children to come and see me!

Monday, 16th. The Uptons rode out with us, and we cantered round the race course, a mile and a half. The 52nd Regiment arrived in the Station yesterday, and they dined at our Mess to-night, H. did not go, nor did we go to the Station Ball, though we had subscribed to it.

Thursday, 19th. We are going into the Dhoon for a month's shooting to-morrow, so I was busy packing up and arranging things H. dined at the Mess, and I with the Bell-Martins. All our things went off in the evening.

Friday, 20th. We were to have set off early this morning, and breakfasted at Malana, but H. altered the arrangements in the morning; he went to Mess, and Mrs. B-M. kindly came over and made me breakfast there. We set off at four, first in the bullock gharie, until the sun had gone down, then we got on our ponies, and rode the rest of the way—in all, eighteen miles. Reached Malana at eight to dinner. Our camp consists of one very large tent, and a smaller one, five camels, a two-bullock hackery, our bullock gharie, two ponies, the red cow and calf, goats, and the dogs. We have lent our other cow to Mrs. Upton while we are away. H. forgot his fishing rod, and sent a coolie for it.

Saturday, 21st The tents etc. were to have left at twelve p.m. but the servants went to sleep, and did not start till half past five, the consequence was, that when we arrived at Billaspoor, no tent was up and the cooking cart was actually behind, so we did not get our cold breakfast until half past two, and the tent was not ready till four. H. shot a duck on the way, but I believe it was not good to eat.

Sunday, 22nd. The things again did not leave in time, and if I had not awoke and made H. call the servants, we should have been as badly off as yesterday. As it was they were not off till nearly three, and when we came to Kidderabad, the tent had not been taken off the camels, and the cooking cart was again behind. However, it soon came up, and we got breakfast, (a hot one this time) at half past eleven, in the tent. The only shade we could find before the tent was up, was the shady side of a large tomb. H. shot a young peacock, and a full snipe. We rode the whole way.

Monday, 23rd. Left Kidderabad early on our ponies, and went round into the jungle. H. only succeeded in shooting a pea hen, an old one too. We reached Kalesur by ten and found everything ready for us, as we had sent the things off at eight last night, which is the only way, for if the men are allowed to go to sleep before starting, they never wake till daylight. In the evening H. went out fishing, and I sat working by the side of the Jumna, and enjoyed it very much. H. caught one fish, of two and a quarter pounds.

Tuesday, 24th. We went out in the morning by the side of the river; we walked a long way, but H. caught nothing. It began to be very hot at two o'clock, at three we dined, and a couple of hours later went on our ponies a long way up the river.

Wednesday, 25th. We left Kalesur at 6 a.m. and rode along such a pretty jungle road. H. took his guns and walked a great part of the way, every now and then turning off into the jungle in search of game, he shot two pea-fowl, which abound here. About three miles from Paunta we came to a deep part of the river, where we stayed more than an hour, and H. caught two fish, one weighing two pounds and the other one pound, we had them for breakfast, they are mahseer and delicious eating, but very full of bones. A large bone stuck in my throat for a quarter of an hour, giving me much pain, and frightening me considerably, as I did not know how long it might choose to remain there, my throat was very painful, for several days afterwards. We went out walking at three, a good way up the river. H. crossed it at the shallowest part, nearly up to his middle, and with a strong current running He caught three small mahseer and one trout. We sent for our ponies and rode back. A coolie came out from Umballah with a letter from John, who has just arrived at Cawnpore with his regiment.

Thursday, 26th. Fishing again, morning and evening, the largest H. caught weighed four pounds. We are much disappointed at the elephants not having arrived, we expected them to join us before this; the jungle is so high there can be no good shooting without them.

Friday, 27th. Not feeling very well I did not accompany H. this morning. He hooked a large fish of five and a quarter pounds, and another of two pounds. At three o'clock H. went out on his pony with five men in search of deer. I rode out at five when it was a little cooler, with two men to take care of me, to try and meet H. coming back, but we missed each other, and he returned to camp sometime before me. I went quite into the jungle, and saw the lair of a tiger, in which there were a number of the bones of deer lying about. As the sun had set I did not feel particularly inclined to stay. Hearing H's rifle I waited about just outside the jungle till, finding it was getting dusk, I rode towards the tents, two miles off, and it was quite dark before I arrived. The report I had heard was caused by H. having discharged his rifle on his return to camp, to have it cleaned! He shot an old buck with fine antlers, and when he came up to it, it was lying apparently dead; he reloaded his gun, and the men were just about to take possession of the animal, when it started up and ran off; they tracked it a long way by its blood, but lost its traces in a nullah—poor thing!

Saturday, 28th. H. went out again this morning to try to find the deer but was unsuccessful, however, he shot and brought back another, she had a fawn with her, but H. assured me that it was quite old enough to eat grass and take care of itself.

In the evening went out but caught no fish, they are beginning to get shy, and unless we go to a fresh place, have little chance of success. H. caught all with an artificial minnow, he tried flies but the fish would not look at them.

[*March*, 1857.]

Tuesday, 3rd. Still at Paunta waiting for the elephants. A coolie came from Umballah and brought three volumes of Macaulay's History of England but no letters, so we do not know whether the elephants are coming or not. We went this afternoon three miles further on, and had our tents pitched close to the river, and H. managed to pull one small fish of about two pounds out of the water

Wednesday, 4th. Mettoo (Kidmutgar) returned from Dehra this morning, with bread and other provisions, he enquired at the Post Office there but found no letters for us. H. went out shooting, but only got a couple of quails.

Thursday, 5th. Went this morning six miles on our way

home, when w earrived we found that the servants had pitched our tent in the middle of the village, surrounded by piles of wood, thatched huts, and cattle. We eat our breakfast, and then, to their great disgust, made them move everything to a place close to the river, about a quarter of a mile from the village. A quantity of logs are collected here and at Paunta, they are cut down in the woods and dragged to the river by bullocks, a log on each side, one end dragging on the ground—this used to frighten our ponies—they are then floated down the river to Delhi, Agra, etc. H. caught five fish in the course of the day.

Friday, 6th. H. shot a turtle and a three-pound fish with his rifle; the turtle was uneatable. We sent off all the things in the evening except the small tent to sleep in and provision for our early cup of tea.

Saturday, 7th. Got up as soon as it was light, had tea and toast, and at half past six set off. The cold was intense, my hands and feet were quite painful from it, and the ground was so wet with dew that I could not dismount and walk to warm myself. We had several stoppages while H. tried to shoot game, but he only succeeded in bagging two pea-fowl which he knocked over with one shot. The road was very hilly and stony so that we were obliged to ride the whole way and it became very hot and I was very unwell. We did not reach the tent at Kidderabad until half-past twelve, to breakfast. Dined at half-past four and at six set off again on horseback. At eight o'clock halted in a nice place, the servants lighted a fire and we made some mulled port, then we sat round the fire until the small tent came up, and we were in bed by ten after a very fatiguing day.

Sunday, 8th. Rode to Billaspoor only about six or eight

miles, where we arrived about nine. A coolie brought a letter from Mrs. Bell-Martin; all our letters, English ones included, had been sent to Dehra. We broke the march by having our tent sent on five or six miles.

Monday, 9th. Came on our ponies to Malana, rode fast and got in by half-past eight. At five we set off again and went six miles to our little tent to tea and sleep.

Tuesday, 10th. Left at half past six, rode very fast and got into Umballah within three hours. Mrs. Bell-Martin came over and sat with me, there have been four or five balls whilst we have been away, and also races. In the evening H. drove me out, and we went to hear the band and to the theatre, where we saw *Naval Engagements,* and *Box and Cox married and settled,* performed by amateurs. The 2nd Fusiliers band played and our soldiers gave us the Ethiopian serenaders between the plays.

Thursday, 12th. H. dined at Mess, and I with the Bell-Martins.

Friday, 13th. I rode out to the Field Day. Very cloudy, and in the night it thundered and lightened with a good deal of rain.

Sunday, 15th. Thunder, lightning and rain last evening and night. I drove Mrs. B-M to church at a quarter to seven, first day of early service. In the evening H. took me for a drive after which English letters came with the sad news of the death of H's mother.

Monday, 16th. Inspection Field day. H. is excused from all duty just now.

Wednesday, 18th. The Commander-in-Chief, General Anson, came into Cantonments, and a salute was fired. At one o'clock he held a Levée, at which all officers have to attend, H. therefore went.

Thursday, 19th. Field day in review order for the inspection of the Commander-in-Chief.

Friday, 20th. H. being Field Officer of the week, went round the guards this morning, and I accompanied him, we rode through the Commander-in-Chief's camp as we knew him to be absent.

Saturday, 21st. Brigade day in review order for all the troops in the station. A grand dinner at Mess, for the Commander-in-Chief, when all the officers of the regiment are in duty bound to go. H. did not return till half past eleven, and was one of the first to leave. I had a little dinner party of the ladies of the regiment.

Monday, 23rd. H. dined with the Commander-in-Chief, and I at Capt. Anson's.

Monday, 30th. H. burnt his hand very badly with phosphorus. He was attempting to write with a piece on the wall in the dark, the friction caused it to explode, he threw it down on the table, which it burnt very much, water not being able to put it out. His hand—or rather his finger and thumb were very much burnt and he was obliged to keep his hand in a basin of water all night.

[*April*, 1857.]

Very unwell, but on the 8th I began to pack the things we shall want in Kashmir. H. has got six months' leave, and my brother has also got leave, and is to go with us, so I hope we shall have a very pleasant trip.

Good Friday, 10th. Cloudy day and some rain. To church in the morning. Finished packing all the things, but the cart did not come to take them away, which, however, was rather fortunate, as they would have been wetted by the rain. We have hired another set of servants to wait on us here, while our old ones go on a-head. I am always ill in the evening from fatigue.

Saturday, 11th. Our things went off in a four-bullock hackery, and we sent on our two ponies and the two dogs. We have laid in a good stock of preserved provisions—tins of biscuits, soups, jam, jellies—six doz. claret, six doz. sherry, two hill tents for ourselves, and one for the servants.

I was very sorry to hear Dr. Tritton had lost his son. He had just got his cadetship, and came out to Calcutta by the February steamer; directly he landed he was taken ill, and died. His parents had not seen him for fourteen years.

Sunday, 12th. At two o'clock this morning I was awakened by the most terrible hurricane I ever heard. In the morning it rained so much that H. had the "dismiss" sounded, and we did not go to church.

Tuesday, 14th. The new General—Sir Henry Barnard arrived in the station yesterday.

Mr. Gifford called on us to say good-bye, he starts to-night for Meerut, to join his new Regiment the Carabineers.

We dined with Capt. and Mrs. Macpherson.

Thursday, 16th. Mrs. Bell-Martin spent the day with me. The husbands dined at Mess to meet Sir Henry Barnard and Brigadiers Johnstone and Hallifax.

Friday, 17th. A little model bedstead has been made by one of the soldiers, at Dr. McAndrews request, and it is to be submitted to Government for approval, to supersede the old kind of beds used in barracks. It is made of iron, folding up in the middle, with canvas laced underneath, which latter part I had the honour of making. The size of the model is an inch to a foot.

I hear there was a fire in one of the uninhabited Infantry Barracks, and a great quantity—several hundred casks—of beer was destroyed. It is supposed to be the work of an incendiary.

It has been a cloudy day, and at six it began to thunder and lighten, and showers of rain continued to fall the whole evening. There was a parade to read about the execution of some Sepoys at Barrackpore, for mutiny. Just after tea, about half past eight, I heard a trumpet sounding at the Barracks, just outside our compound, no unusual thing in itself, but I remarked to H. it was a call I had never heard, presently it sounded all through the lines —the alarm of fire; and horses were heard galloping about in all directions. H. instantly put on his uniform, ordered his horse and went out, having first given directions for the Fire Brigade, and a Patrol etc. I went over to the Bell-Martin's bungalow just opposite, not caring to be left alone in the house. The fire was in an empty house in the Native Infantry lines, and it was totally destroyed. At half past ten H. returned, and we went home to bed.

Saturday, 18th. At 3.15 this morning, I was awakened by the alarm of fire. H. at once got up and went off, I also got up, and am now writing this feeling safer, dressed, than if I were in bed.

These continued fires are supposed to be the work of the Sepoys (or Sepahis), amongst whom there is great disaffection in many parts. At Barrackpore, one Brahmin was hanged, and several have been sentenced to fourteen years transportation. The 19th N.I. at that place has been disbanded.

Saturday evening. This last fire was in the Sikh lines where several huts were burnt. H. returned at five, we laid down for half an hour, but I did not sleep. Had tea, and H. went to the Brigade Field Day. I walked in the garden, and after my sleepless night, I did not sleep in the day or feel very tired.

Another Parade in the evening. H. has a great deal to do just now, being in command of the Regiment, as Colonel Grant has gone to have some tiger shooting. Mrs. Grant is staying with her sister, Mrs. Shakespear, at Bignor. H. is also Field Officer of the week, and is therefore obliged to attend any little disturbances in the Station. Brigadier Hallifax thinks a storm is brewing, and those at a distance think more of it than we in the station do.

We heard this morning of poor Colonel Pratt's* death, he died shortly after going on board ship.

Sunday, 19th. Very early this morning, Colonel Yule came to say one of our men had been stabbed in barracks during the night. H. and I went to church this morning. We have not heard from J. for two months, though I have written to him several times, asking for an immediate answer. I was getting alarmed, so we sent him a telegraphic message to Cawnpore, and the answer was he intends starting on the 21st, and hopes to reach this in five days, therefore, we may expect him by next Sunday.

At 8.30 this evening there was the usual alarm of fire, H. went to see about it, it was an officer's stables, which were completely destroyed.

An enquiry was made about the man stabbed. He stated that a native came into the barracks, and stabbed him in three places, but they did not succeed in capturing the man; it turned out, however, that the soldier had stabbed himself to create a sensation. The holes in his shirt and flannel did

*Captain and Brevet Lt. Colonel 9th Lancers.

not correspond with his wounds, and had evidently been made afterwards!

Monday, 20th. At 12 o'clock last night a soldier came to say there was another fire. H. went to see where it was, and found it was a Police Chokee, two miles distant. As he was returning, he had to go to another fire, which burnt a native officer's house. He came back about 2 o'clock this morning. I am quite knocked up by the disturbed and sleepless nights we have had lately.

Tuesday, 21st. No alarm of fire during the night, but this morning it was reported to H., as field officer of the week, that an attempt had been made to burn a hut of the 5th N.I. Some gunpowder tied up in a bit of rag was found in the thatch, but the smoke was perceived, and the ball removed before it had taken effect.

General Sir H. Barnard called here to-day with Brigadier Hallifax. I drove Mrs. Bell-Martin to hear the band, H. was as usual engaged all the evening on duty.

Wednesday, 22nd. We were awakened again by fire. H. sent to know where it was, and one of the picket soon came to say it was five huts of the 60th N.I. that had been burnt, and the fire extinguished, so H. did not get up.

I went with H. round the guards; formerly the Field Officer, and Captain of the week were only obliged to visit the guards once each during their tour of duty, now there is an order issued that one or the other must go round them daily.

Thursday, 23rd. No alarm of fire, but I heard there was one near the city, and also that an attempt had been made to ignite Major Laughton's* stables. H. went to Mess, and I dined with the Uptons.

Saturday, 25th. No fire occurred last night, or the night

*Bengal Engineers.

before. H. drove me to the Band. Colonel Mowatt* came up and talked to me, and afterwards I had a long conversation with Sir Henry Barnard*. If everything is quiet, he thinks Lady Barnard and his daughter will come out to India in the cold weather. He introduced his son and A. D. C., Capt. Barnard to me, and finished by buying our Buggy.

Sunday, 26th. Last night at eleven, we heard that there was a fire close to us, it looked just as if it was our fine Mess house. The trumpet fire alarm was sounded as H. had ordered, only, if there was a fire in our own lines. H. soon dressed, and I got up and sat in the verandah, from where I could plainly see the fire blazing furiously ; all the engines attended but they did not succeed in putting it out, the scarcity of water being the obstacle, it has to be pulled up from wells by bucketfuls at a time. It turned out to be our band-master's house, just on the other side of the Mess house, and very close to it. H. had the engines played on the roof to prevent it from catching fire, as there was a very high wind blowing, and the Brigade Major, Mr. Simpson, had his things taken out of his house, and all ready for a start, in case his Bungalow should take fire. Poor Mr. Anton succeeded in saving all his things, but no persuasion could make him go to a friend's house, he insisted on staying in the compound, and sat down disconsolately in the middle of his effects, to take care of them.

H. returned at two, and at four o'clock we were told the "Sahib" had arrived, H. went to him, and I dressed as quickly as possible, and went to welcome my dearest brother, after a separation of twelve years and eight months. At six we all went to lie down a little, and rest ourselves.

*Both of these Officers died within two months, from anxiety and exposure.

One of Mr. Shaw's* outhouses was set on fire, and Mr. Evan's* thatch caught fire, but he succeeded in putting it out, before any mischief was done. H. has ordered a picket to be on duty in the 9th Lancer lines, and to arrest any native in them between nine o'clock in the evening and dawn. J. drove me to church in the morning.

Monday, 27th. J. took me for a drive in the Cavalry lines, he drives very well considering he has only one hand to manage with† but I was always rather alarmed at turning corners.

H. has laid our Dâk to Bhimber for the 4th, instead of the 1st of May, that we may see a little more of dear J. as he cannot go with us. He had got his six months' leave all right, but the day before he left, he received a letter offering him the appointment of Brigade-Major at Cawnpore, during the absence of the present one on sick leave. This (J. said) put him into "a great passion" and he wanted to send a refusal of the offer, but his friends persuaded him not to refuse, so he wrote and said if they would give him leave till the 1st of June he would accept it, and he started for Umballah without waiting for an answer, but he received it here acceding to his terms.‡

Friday, 30th. H. and J. called on the General, Brigadier etc. In the evening J. and I walked to the church, they were putting up the punkahs, and it looked quite fit for service; we then walked to the soldiers' gardens, sat down on one of the benches, and had a nice talk of old times, and went home rather tired.

H. and J. dined at Mess, I at the Bell-Martins. H. has made my brother a knife and fork in one, to enable him to cut and eat his dinner more readily.

*9th Lancers.
†He lost his arm at the battle of Chillianwallah.
‡ His visit to us happily saved him from going through the Cawnpore horrors.

[*May*, 1857.]

Saturday, 2nd. J. drove me to the band. I had a headache all the afternoon.

Sunday, 3rd. I tried to get up to go to church, but was obliged to go to bed again, I felt so ill. J. had promised to go with me, and we were to have received the Holy Communion together, but he also was taken ill in the night.

Last evening Dr. Clifford came and talked to us at the Band, I was observing it did not seem so good as usual, and he said it was without its head, the cornopean player was ill in hospital. This morning, H. told me he had died during the night of Asiatic cholera. Both J. and myself were very unwell all day.

Monday, 4th. Colonel Grant called in the morning. I was so ill, I was quite unfit to do anything. Mrs. Upton came and helped me, and she and her husband breakfasted and dined with us. Of course there was an immense deal to do giving up our house, etc. and everything seemed left till the last day. How it was all got through I am sure I do not know; most of the furniture, crockery, etc. was lent to Mrs. Upton, the gharie was sent for Mrs. Bell-Martin's use, and I gave her my goats. I felt so miserable, principally I suppose from having to leave my dear brother just as we were beginning to know each other again, after so long a separation. The Bell-Martins and Mrs. Grant came in towards evening, and just at the last I had to pay all the servants, and my head was in such confusion, and there were so many people present, that I was quite bewildered. I never in all my life passed such a day, and I hope never to have to pass through such another.

We left in our Dhoolies about eight in the evening, and J. came on and wished us good bye again when we had gone a few yards. He is to dine with the Grindalls, sleep at the Hotel, and breakfast at the Uptons; he starts for Mussourie to-morrow evening, where he intends staying till it is time to join his appointment, as Brigade-Major at Cawnpore, on the 1st. of June. H. gave him his first charger, a grey Arab, he will require one, as a mounted officer.*

Tuesday, 5th. Forty miles to Khana Ka Serai, arrived at nine o'clock this morning, slept little. Found after I had taken particular trouble about the bread, that it had been left behind, so that we have to eat Chupatties. Also H. insisted on packing the wine etc. himself, and I was annoyed to find that the beer which we never drink and which I had intended for J. had been put in by mistake, and we have one dozen of soda water, and twelve bottles of claret for six days consumption. Used a punkah and tatties.†

Wednesday, 6th. Reached Loodiana at two o'clock a.m. three chokies or 30 miles, which was very quick travelling but the road is good.

There used to be a large station here formerly, but on account of the great mortality amongst the troops, it has been almost abandoned, and there are now only a few Irregulars here. I remember J. being stationed at this place, soon after coming to India, and that he had a very severe illness. A cooler day, the thermometer never above 86° in doors.

We started about 7 o'clock in the evening. Loodiana appears a large place, and we passed a number of fine look-

*This charger was lost going down country
†Kus-kus matting hung before the doors and windows and kept wet.

ing buildings, and a fort, built apparently on a raised platform. We also passed a splendid bridge, not yet completed, and a few miles further on crossed the Sutlej on a bridge of boats, on nearly every one of which there was a small hut. This river is three miles wide in the rains. About eight miles from Loodiana is Phillour, a fine looking town, with a fort built of stone. There is also a Cantonment here.

Thursday, 7th. A very pleasant dâk, nice cool air, but I slept little. We reached Jellunder at gun-fire, about half past four; the coolies took us first to a miserable hotel, but we came on to the Dâk Bungalow. We were ten hours going only two miles more than we did yesterday in seven. We got some capital strawberries, far the best I have seen or tasted in India, nearly as good as English ones. I feel much better to-day, yesterday I was very unwell and quite unable to do anything.

Friday, 8th. We had no sun after four, on account of the cloudiness of the sky, we took advantage of it, and set off at five last evening, as we had a sixty miles dâk before us, but the thermometer in the dhoolie showed 98°, and there being no breeze, the heat was very oppressive. Towards morning it fell to 76°, but by the time we reached the staging Bungalow at Umritzer at 8.30, it had risen to 97° on the shady side of the Dhoolie, and I had a racking head-ache, which, however, went off after breakfast, I never enjoyed a cup of tea so much. I slept nearly all night, having been almost entirely without sleep the night before, and I rarely sleep in the day time. I have some faint idea of crossing rivers—it was the Beas, there was a great deal of sand in the middle, so we had to go twice in a boat.

Saturday, 9th. We started very early last night as we

expected to go straight to Goojeranwalla upwards of sixty miles, however, just as we were starting our bearers told us that our dâk was laid to Lahore, only about thirty miles so we might have waited till the thermometer was less than 98°. On waking in the night from the bearers putting me down close to the other Dhoolie, I spoke to H. but receiving no answer, supposed he was asleep. I then saw the Dhoolie was going the other way, which frightened me, as I fancied the bearers were playing some trick, when a strange gentleman's voice behind answered one of my questions, "I think this must be a Chokee, and that we have changed bearers" On looking in front I saw H's Dhoolie some distance ahead, and when I came up he said we had not passed a Chokee for some time, so I suspect my bearers and that gentleman's must have changed in order to save themselves the ten miles return journey. We reached Lahore at three o'clock, and had a good sleep till seven. Saw Colonel Yule's name in the Bungalow book as having left last night.

It was too hot to go out and see any of the sights of Lahore, but I hope when we return the Arnolds will be there.

Sunday, 10th. We left at six last night, and passed outside the walls of Lahore, which looked so pretty with its numerous buildings, domes, and minarets peeping out from between the trees, the city is entirely surrounded by a fine looking wall and bastions. A few miles on we crossed the Ravee, which in the dry weather is separated into three streams, the first and last we crossed by a bridge of boats, the middle one was not knee deep. The bridge keeper said a rupee to pay. H. called for the book, it was eight annas, just half, the natives cannot help cheating. I am beginning to get accustomed to Dâk travelling, and slept very well the whole night after the first stage. The night felt very cold, the thermometer sank to 72°.

We arrived at Goojeranwalla at 6 o'clock. The Dâk Bungalow is constructed out of the gate way to the garden belonging to the tomb of Runjeet Singh, who was buried here; he died just before the fall of Lahore. Thermometer 87° at 12 noon.

Monday, 11th. We left Goojeranwalla at 6.30 last night, and reached Goojerat at 4 this morning. The Dâk Bungalow is an old Sikh Serai, fitted up as a staging bungalow, it looked worse than it proved to be, for the thermometer was not higher than usual which is 88° at the warmest time of the day. I was very unwell with palpitations whenever I sat up, and I experienced very great drowsiness. No bread to be got here, only chupatties, made of common brown ottah.

Tuesday, 12th. We reached Bhimber at four o'clock this morning, nine and a half hours on the road. Our servants and tents were all right, and had been here more than a week. Colonel Yule, who arrived yesterday, was just going to set off; we got coolies as quickly as we could, and at half past five, were on our way, having merely had a cup of coffee, with very bad milk, and a biscuit. We left our dhoolies with the head man of the village, until our return. The road was dreadful, my little pony carried me very well, but I preferred walking, with the risk of tiring myself, when the hill was so very steep, and over a stratum of slate, for I was afraid the pony would slip, and fall, it seemed almost as risky as going over ice. A few miles further on we came up to Colonel Yule, who was stopping on the road to breakfast. I threw myself quite exhausted on a heap of hay; the heat and exertion of climbing so steep a hill, had parched my mouth and throat, and I was thankful for some of Colonel Yule's tea, though without milk, and afterwards he gave me some grilled chicken and chupatties. We then proceeded on a little way, stopping now and then in a shady place to rest. From Vigne's account, we thought the first march was over a good road, so that we could ride fast all the way, or I should have had my dandy* with me. A man brought some wild yellow raspberries, with which we refreshed ourselves. H. gave a man a two-anna piece for giving us a little water, he was quite disatisfied, and said he ought to have a rupee. The grass-cut in charge of my pony who was carrying H's revolver, and walking a little way behind me, let it go off through carelessness, or H. said curiosity—fortunately the bullet did not hit me.

We reached the Serai at three o'clock, it is a miserable place, mud walls, uneven earthen floors, and open door ways. We find great difficulty in procuring coolies, they do not like coming, many people do not pay them, or only an anna a piece. Several of our things were left behind, amongst them, our tent pegs, so that we could not have our tents pitched, and were obliged to use one of these rooms, swarm-

ing with fleas, and very hot at night. Of course there is no furniture in these Serais, nothing but the bare walls. Colonel Yule dined with us.

A gentleman passed us on the road this morning, leading a fine horse down the hill, and I thought a pony would have been more useful.

*A long pole, with a carpet slung to it, much like a hammock, in which I sit or lie, and it is carried by two men at a time.

Wednesday, 13th. I scarcely slept at all. Up early, tea, and off by five. Colonel Yule sets off before four, walks the whole way, and drinks no wine or beer, only tea. I had my dandy carried by me, and made good use of it. We passed Colonel Yule sitting on a high rock, waiting for his breakfast, we went up for a few minutes to admire the view, which included the snowy summits of the Pir Punjal. A few miles further on, we stopped for breakfast, and arrived at Naushaira at 10 a.m. Thermometer 88° at 12 o'clock. This is rather a better place than the last, being situated in a garden. Colonel Yule dined with us, and played backgammon with me. I am suffering very much from pain in my back, from riding up-hill so much, and very probably got cold afterwards.

Thursday, 14th. Colonel Yule went on this morning, we remained, as three or four of our boxes, and two servants, had not been seen since we left Bhimber, they arrived in the evening. H. went out in the morning to fish, but caught nothing, he was more successful in the evening, hauling up three good sized fish. I had my back rubbed by the Ayah, with half a wineglass of brandy, and a quantity of red pepper, it made my back burn so dreadfully afterwards, it very much resembled what I should fancy might be the sensation of being roasted before a slow fire. We heard the cuckoo's note for the first time.

Friday, 15th. Woke at a little before four, got up, had tea, and were on our way by half past four. The Kotwāl of the village behaved very badly, he was a great talker and said we should have as many coolies and ponies as we required. We started before our things, and H. gave him a letter, some fishing tackle, and a present of money. After three and a half hours travelling, we stopped for breakfast, but the servants and coolies had not arrived, and did not make their appearance for nearly two hours. Our servants told us that directly we left, the Kotwāl, and all the coolies went away, so they had to go into the village and seize some coolies to carry our boxes. The road was exceedingly pretty, but very bad, and I found my Dandy most useful, H. was very tired, from being obliged to walk so much. We arrived at our tent at Chungus Serai, at half past two, just in time to escape getting wet through; it was only a thunder shower. This is a small place, and to my delight there is no Serai, we had our tents pitched on a pretty, grassy lawn, by the side of a little stream. H. went a long way in the evening, but got no fish. We saw a number of fire flies.

Saturday, 16th. We left early, and came along a very pretty road, we had to cross and recross a wide and rapid river, three or four times. H. took off his shoes and socks and waded through, the water was much above his knees, and very cold, as we are getting near the snow. We reached Rajouri, at half past two, having as usual breakfasted on the way. This was a very long march. We found Colonel Yule here, and we dined together. My back is still very painful, so that I cannot sit up to write, without pain.

Sunday, 17th. We did not set off until nearly six; very few coolies to be obtained, and most of them old men, to whom we could only give half a load, one man had only a small charpoy, (bedstead) and a mattrass, he fell down and broke the bedstead in pieces; he was rather afraid to come up to be paid, but H. assured him he should get his money, and also gave him a spoonful of Curacoa, as he looked so thin and weak. We arrived at Tanna at three, and found Colonel Yule sitting in the shade. His tent was soon put up, and he made me go into it, but, after some time, as our things had not appeared, and I did not like keeping him so long out of his little tent, we got him to have his servants' *Sholdaree* pitched for us—such a nice one.

Some of our effects arrived about six o'clock, others later, and many did not come at all that night. We dined together, borrowing Colonel Yule's little table, and using a couple of boxes for chairs. One bedstead being broken, and the other not having arrived, we were obliged to sleep on the ground in our small tent, the whole of the other not being here, fortunately, we had all our bedding. This is a hot place, although it is about 5,000 feet above the level of the sea.

Monday, 18th. The remainder of our things came this morning, with the Sirdar-bearer. I was very unwell during the night. We halted, but had our encampment removed to a better place—a small grassy plain, just large enough for our tents, surrounded by streams of water.

The trouble we have about coolies is very great, and we made a mistake in having heavy boxes instead of kilters or baskets. Sometimes our cases of wine, etc., do not come in till late at night, or early the next morning, often with four men to carry three dozen bottles, or even less; and they very often put their load down in the road and run off, when the servants in charge have to go and seek fresh coolies. Between fifty and sixty men stand round the tent, making such a noise—wanting their money, that they may go away. Now, if we happen to be at a place where we cannot obtain fresh coolies, we dare not pay them in full, but just give them enough to get some food, until we reach a place where we can procure others, then we pay them up, and let them go, otherwise, they would all be off directly they got their money, and we should be left in the lurch; as it is, many of them prefer going without their pay, to accompanying us another march. It seems hard to oblige them to carry our luggage, whether they wish it or not, but what can we do? We had some of our wine boxes cut in two, so that they might be carried like kilters, also I have had a kind of janpan—as it is called—made for me like the native women travel in, it is short, like a small bedstead cut in half, I am even with the men's shoulders, and am obliged to sit like a tailor, with my legs crossed.

Tuesday, 19th. We set off early, about five o'clock, I in my janpan with six men, and H. as usual. The road—which word must always be understood as the way, for there is no real road, the path being generally the dry, and sometimes even the wet bed of a water course—this march was three miles up a very steep hill, finely wooded, and three miles down hill, when we had to cross a roaring torrent, by a little bridge, composed of two rough planks or trees, thrown across at some little height above the torrent, on which small branches are fastened, and through which you can see the water flowing underneath your feet. The bridge is very narrow, and without any protection on either side. We heard that the gentleman who passed us on the first march from Bhimber, lost his fine horse here, its foot went through, and in trying to extricate itself, slipped, fell over into the torrent, and was drowned. Goolab Singh's Prime Minister is travelling here from Kashmir, and has caused all the bridges to be repaired, and the snow cleared from the Pir Panjal Pass. We met one of his wives travelling in a dhoolie—he himself has gone another way—I went up and spoke to her, she did not strike me as at all pretty, but she had a fine little boy by her side, with such beautiful eyes.

After crossing the bridge, which we did on foot, we ascended a very high hill to Burrumgullah, where our tents were pitched, at about two o'clock. Though I travelled in a recumbent position the whole way, I was very tired and knocked up on my arrival, and indeed I have been very unwell for a long time.

On the first hill from Tanna, most beautiful flowers grew, amongst which I noticed the Barberry, two kinds of Jasmine—yellow and white, etc.

We shall not see Colonel Yule again until we get to Kashmir, as he goes by Punch and we by the Pir Panjal; he does not intend to stay long at Sirinugger, but to travel about the Hills beyond and return to Umballah by Chini and Simla.*

Wednesday, 20th. Rose at 4.30 and at 5.0 set off, the morning was very cold. As the road was very hilly, H. had four men to carry him in the Dandy. We passed a splendid waterfall, I should like to know its height, it must have been something very great, and the column of water was tremendous, I got quite wet with the spray, although I kept at a great distance from it† Our path lay along the side of the torrent which we crossed and re-crossed thirty times in all! sometimes a branch of the torrent had to be waded across, or a piece of wood or log of a tree the width of a man's foot, joined the banks; at one place the way was blockaded by a huge mass of snow, when my men had to climb with me over the trunks of huge fallen trees, and finally up a perpendicular bank, when, if they had missed their footing I should have been precipiated into the torrent below. I certainly was rather alarmed, and offered to get out and climb though I think I should have found it rather an impossibility. The ponies had to be unsaddled

*We never saw him again; he was killed shortly after joining the Regiment.
†The height is about 70 feet.

and led across the torrent, one man holding the bridle and another the tail of the animal, as it was impossible for even our hill ponies to ascend such a place. After this we had to traverse some snow which had fallen over the torrent, forming a kind of bridge. The scenery was indescribably grand. We bought two sheep before starting, one for ourselves and servants, the other for the coolies, and we did not omit, as the custom is, to give the head to the Fakīr of the Pir Panjal. For four days we have never been out of the sound of falling water, to-day our tent is pitched far above it, on a grassy plain close to a precipice abruptly descending to the torrent. To-morrow we cross the Pir Panjal. I have managed to get a very bad cold and cough.

Thursday, 21st. Here we are on the Pir Panjal, and I am sitting with one of H's. very warm great coats on over a thick shawl, in fact I have put on every wrap I could find, the weather is so intensely cold, and I can hardly write my fingers are so frigid.

We set off as usual about five, and after going a little way up hill we made a very precipitous descent into the valley, before beginning the ascent of the Pir Panjal which was very steep. We breakfasted at the top which it took us more than than three hours to reach. A great part of the way was over snow, and all the men were shod with plaited cord tied on their feet to prevent them from slipping. This pass is very nearly 12,000 feet above the sea's level. We went for some distance at this elevation between two very high peaks; I wore a veil to protect my eyes from the glare of the snow.

We met an officer on the road who is going as quickly as possible to join his regiment; he spoke to H. and told him that the Indian army is in a state of mutiny; that one regiment had risen and murdered the Colonel, and several other regiments had been disbanded. A little further on we met another gentleman, he told us all officers have orders to join their regiments except those who have families with them. I do not know whether this applies to Queen's or only to Company's officers. Our tents were pitched on a pretty grassy plain; soon after we arrived we had a storm of thunder and lightning. In the evening two more officers came, and pitched their tents at a little distance off. H. gave them a couple of bottles of beer, which they said they had not tasted since they left their regiments. I forgot to say that at Poshiana, as there was no ground available for our tents, we were obliged to have them pitched on the roofs of houses.

Friday, 22nd. Rose early, but did not leave Allahabad till nearly six, we stayed to see all the coolies set off, there were between sixty and seventy of them. The way for the most part lay along the side of the mountain, and there is not much ascent, or descent, but it was a long march. Another gentleman passed when our tents were up at Hurripoor, he came in and had a glass of wine, and a biscuit; he had only got as far as Shupeyon (the next march from here), and was obliged to turn back, without getting even a sight of Sirinugger. Soon after our arrival, a most terrible storm of wind and dust came on, and we were afraid the tent would not stand such violence. The thermometer sank to 59° outside, and it was only 62° inside the tent.

Saturday, 23rd. Dressed at a little after four, and off at five. This early rising these cold mornings does not improve my cough and cold, and my chest was very painful. When we first set off, I wrap a warm blanket round me, and when the sun has risen, and it becomes warm, the blanket is transferred to the top of my janpan, to which it forms the top and curtains. I am always very sorry when it is time to put it up, as it impedes my view very much. We met three officers of the 81st (Queen's) returning to their regiment, and H. learnt from them that all the ladies had left Kashmir, and gone back by way of Murray. H. still determines to proceed to the city, and return another way, as he feels sure I could not exist through such another journey as we have had. Our path lay along the valley; Shupeyon is a beautiful place, and there is a very nice encamping ground, on a fine lawn, shaded by beautiful trees, a rapid river flows close by, and the range of snowy mountains a short distance beyond, forms a splendid back-ground to the picture. We ought to have come to this place yesterday, but halted by mistake at Hurripoor, only five miles distant.

We get such tiny chickens here that I think nothing of eating a whole one at dinner, or breakfast, they are very good, and only cost an anna (three half-pence) a piece.

Sunday, 24th. Cannot halt, obliged to hurry on. H. forgot to wind up his watch, but I could see it was later than usual when we set off, At first our path lay through rice fields, and we were continually crossing little streams of water, afterwards we went over a plain covered with the finest and greenest grass, just like a gentleman's well-kept lawn in England; and there were such pretty flowers—the white and lilac Iris being abundant, and beautiful double yellow roses, but these had a disagreeable scent. We breakfasted about three miles on the road. When we reached Mornpoor, it appeared such a short march, that we ordered merely a rest, and then went on, promising the coolies extra payment.

We traversed the most beautiful country, it was really worth all the trouble and fatigue of the journey, just to see it. It rather reminded me of some of the prettiest parts of Devonshire, with the great advantage of the beautiful snowy range for a back-ground. We rested often, that our baggage might get in front, and came at last to a large river, which we had to cross in boats; getting our horses and luggage over, of course delayed us a long time. As I believe this river goes to Sirinugger, we endeavoured to procure some boats to take us there, but the inhabitants of the village would not let us have any, although there were numbers of them to be seen. We went two or three miles further on, and came to another river which we crossed by a good bridge, and here we were able to hire three boats, one for ourselves, another for the table servants and cooking establishment, and a third, very large one, for our luggage, and the rest of the servants, but most of our things being behind, we were obliged to stay the night here. Islamabad is about three miles further up the river, we hope to see it on our return. Captain Sanctuary's tent was pitched on the opposite side of the river, H. went across and had a long talk with him, hearing more news and particulars. All the troops at Delhi rose, murdered their officers, and all the Christian inhabitants of the town, sacked the Treasury, and burnt the bridge. The officer in command of the powder magazine, blew it up with himself and five hundred Sepoys—so goes the story—I trust it is very much exaggerated. All who managed to escape, fled to Umballah.

Our regiment has marched towards Delhi, and forces are being concentrated, but surely it will be death to Europeans to march about, and live in tents this weather, in the plains, it is the hottest month of the whole year.

The two Sepoy regiments at Umballah, the 5th and the 60th have been disbanded, so Captain Sanctuary* has no longer any regiment to join; however, he goes to report himself at Sealkote. We dined and slept in our boat.

Monday, 25th. Our things not having arrived this morning, we started, leaving our luggage boat to follow us. It is such a pleasant change floating down the stream without any fatigue. We have four men to help the boat on with paddles, which look very much like wooden spoons on a large scale. We breakfasted about nine, and shortly after met some boats, and seeing an English lady and gentleman, we rowed over to them, and found they were Captain and Mrs. Synge, of the 52nd Queen's Infantry, very sorry to be obliged to leave Kashmir, after having only been there ten days. They were going to Ismalabad, and over the Pir Panjal, they had come by the Punch road. In the evening we reached Sirinugger. H. went to look for a house, and was caught in a tremendous storm—thunder, lightning, and rain, so we thought it better to remain in our boat for the night, than to go to an empty house with our bedsteads and furniture behind.

Tuesday, 26th. At half past five in the morning we took possession of our house, one of several built by the Maharajah for the accommodation of the English visiting Kashmir, it was the only one vacant. There are no doors or windows in it, only open places, with a lattice of wood for the window of the principal room, there are no fire-places, and the floors are composed of earth. If we were going to stay here, I daresay we could make ourselves tolerably comfortable. Our house is one of the very few not on the banks of the river, which is rather an advantage in some respects, more private, though not so pretty. I am

*5th B.N.I. He was killed shortly afterwards.

so weak and ill, that I could scarcely walk from the boat to the house, though it was only about two hundred yards. The doctor came to see me this morning. There are two ladies still in Kashmir, Capt. and Mrs. Ximenes, 8th Regiment (Queen's), he is on sick leave, and Capt. and Mrs. Thomas (27th Queen's), he is laid up with a bad foot. There seem to be a number of gentlemen, I believe on sick certificate.

The Maharajah, Goolab Singh, sent us a present of two sheep, a couple of fowls, flour, a little tea, spices, etc. Provisions here are wonderfully cheap, a sheep costs eight annas, (equal to about one shilling); fowls, two annas each; small ones, one anna; ducks, three to four annas.

Dr. Clement Smith came to see me again in the evening, and the next morning breakfasted with us, and gave H. a certificate of my health to send to Colonel Grant, saying he considered me quite incapable of travelling at present. I received a letter from J., he dates from Mussouri, May 16th. The people there are very much alarmed, the gentlemen mount guard, and he had been in command the night before, and was very sleepy in consequence.

Thursday, 28th. H. took some photographs on the river and in the afternoon called on Goolab Singh, who came down the river in his boat to meet him, and they talked together for a long time—in Hindustani. His son Runjeet Singh was present.

H. brought back a *Lahore Extra* with him, the news is more alarming. The Nussuri Battalion (Major Bagot's Goorkha Regiment) turned rebellious, the people at Simla were in fear of their lives, and all assembled at the Bank. Lord William Hay it is said has come to terms with them, giving them two months' advance (or arrears?) of pay, and allowing them again to guard the Treasury, with several other things they demanded.

The paper also gave the list of those murdered at Meerut (which happened before the massacre at Delhi), and amongst them I see the name of Cornet McNab, of the 3rd Cavalry, (native) who had but lately joined, and had been staying with Mrs. Grant, of whom he is a distant connection.

Saturday, 30th. I am able to go out in the boat, being carried down to it in my janpan, and to-day we started after an early breakfast to see the Shalimar gardens. Dr. Smith came with us, it took us two hours to get there, we turned off from the principal stream, and went down a lovely river, and through some great flood gates, which close of their own accord when there is too much water in the river, so as to prevent the lake and valley from being flooded. In the middle of the lake is a small island, with some very fine chunar (oriental plane) trees, from which it takes its name. We landed there for a few minutes, and regaled ourselves with ripe mulberries. There was formerly a building here, but Goolab Singh caused it to be destroyed, and the stone to be carried away for other purposes, which is a great pity, for it must have been a beautiful little spot; it is now quite overgrown with low jungle. We passed close to the far-famed floating gardens, they are composed of the weeds cut from the lake, which float to the surface, and upon this, soil is placed, they are then anchored to the bottom of the lake. We then proceeded to the Shalimar or Royal gardens, on the other side of the lake; the building itself is handsome, supported by pillars of black marble beautifully carved at the base, the verandah is edged with the same. The ceiling is composed of small pieces of painted wood, formed into a pattern; the walls have been plastered over, but in places where the plaster has fallen away, painting in a running pattern may be seen. The building stands in the middle of a square reservoir, and the water descends from it into the lake by a narrow canal, and falls over an artificial cascade at three ornamental buildings or lodges, which are supported by marble pillars.

We had our dinner in the shady verandah, where it was very cool and pleasant, and after some songs to the guitar, began our return journey.

I should not have believed it, had anyone told me when, as a girl, I read Moore's Lalla Rookh, that I should one day stand in the very palace where Moore makes her discover, in the poet Feramorz, the young sovereign of Bochara, whom she has come from Delhi to wed.

On our way back we saw two large fires on the banks of the river. On enquiry, we were told they were dead bodies undergoing the process of cremation. H. made me get out of the boat to look at them, but I could not distinguish them from the logs of burnt wood, and I was nearly blown away and blinded by a sudden and tremendous storm of wind and dust. They were the bodies of a man and a little child; babies dying at a few months old are merely thrown into the river—they are not cremated until they are about two years old.

Sunday, 31st. I did not go out to-day. H. went in the evening to a review of the Maharajah's troops which takes place every Sunday; he seemed pleased with it.

[*June*, 1857.]

Monday, 1st. I am better, and we hope to be able to leave in a day or two. In the evening we went in the boat to a shawl manufactory. H. insisted on my having the handsomest cloak there, one worked all over of "Lady Gomm's" pattern; he also ordered two little cloaks for Mary and Harrie,* but they will not be ready for some time as they have to be made. On the way we met Goolab Singh and his son taking an airing in their large boat. There were an immense number of rowers, but they were ill-dressed and dirty. An *extra* was sent us; things look bad; the 9th Lancers are no longer at Umballah; troops from there are marching to Delhi, also another column, including the Carabineers, from Meerut, and this in the very hottest time of the whole year, just before the rains commence. H. does not know what to do, of course he is most anxious to be with his regiment, but he does not like leaving me alone. Goolab Singh told H. if he would leave me under his protection he would take the greatest care of me, but I would much rather die on the road. It would be much easier to join the regiment from England than from here. We were very sorry to hear that the Commander-in-Chief, General Anson, died of cholera, at Umballah.

Thursday, 4th. I did not go out all day. I am too weak to go anywhere except in the boat where I can lie down all the time. H. very restless and excited, not knowing what to do. I made him take a ride in the evening, thinking it would do him more good than going in the boat. Some gentleman lent us a newspaper; most of the ladies have left Umballah and gone to Kussowlie; those who remain sleep in the Hospital of the 9th Lancers, which is fortified. The new church is also barricaded. H. sent to Goolab Singh, to request permission to go through the Jummo pass, but he made some excuse.†

*Nieces.

† Had we gone by the Jummoo Pass we should have had to pass through Sealkote, and should have arrived just at the very time that the massacre happened. "The

Saturday, 6th. H. went with the Doctor up the Tukt-i-Suliman (or throne of Solomon*), which is a high hill, rising abruptly from the plain, quite close to the city. At its summit is an old building, from whence there must be a very good view of the city and surrounding country.

The valley of Kashmir is about 90 miles in length, and the river which flows through it is nearly 200 yards wide.

The bridge over the river is very picturesque. Trunks of trees are driven into the river at intervals, stones are then thrown in all round them, on these are placed more trunks, the longest being placed at the top, timbers are laid on these, and not covered with any soil. Houses and shops are built on it.

Sunday, 7th. The Baboo brought us an *Extra* of the 30th of May. The mutineers marched out of Delhi, and attacked Brigadier Wilson's Column, but were well beaten, and the Brigadier captured four pieces of heavy ordnance, a twenty-four pounder howitzer, a large quantity of ammunition, and entrenching tools. Wilson's force was about 1,000 strong, and was *en route* from Meerut to join the Umballah force. It is announced that all the Europeans at Hansi and Hissar have been massacred.

Colonel Mowatt (Bengal Artillery), died of cholera in camp, and Brigadier Hallifax had a sun-stroke, and has

Mutiny at Sealkote took place on the 9th of July. It lay in proximity to the Jummoo territory of the Maharajah of Cashmere, who the Sepoys believed, and our authorities feared would, in the hour of danger, forsake his alliance; and it was utterly without any defence of European troops. As ever, the Cavalry were foremost in the work of mutiny,—foremost in their greed for blood. Mounted on good chargers, they could ride with rapidity from place to place, and follow the white men on horseback or in their carriages, and shoot them down as they rode. A ball from the pistol of a mounted trooper entered the broad back of the Brigadier (Brind), and he was carried to the Fort only to die. The Superintending Surgeon, Graham, was shot dead in his buggy, as his daughter sat by his side. Another medical officer of the same name was "killed in his carriage among his children." A Scotch missionary, named Hunter, on his way to the Fort in a carriage, with his wife and child, was attacked by some Chuprassies of the gaol-guard, and all three were ruthlessly murdered. The Brigade-Major, Captain Bishop, was killed in the presence of his family, under the very walls of the Fort. Some hid themselves during the day, and escaped discovery and death almost by a miracle." A HISTORY OF THE SEPOY WAR IN INDIA, by J. W. Kaye, F.R.S., 2nd vol., page 626.

* So called by the Mussulmans, or Sir-i-Shur—Siva's heart—by the Hindoos.

been sent back to Umballah. The troopers of the 8th Light Cavalry, at Mean Meer, have been deprived of their horses as a precautionary measure.

Monday, 8th. The Maharajah's little grandson came to see us, and H. gave him a knife of mine, one of those containing so many useful things. He is a nice little boy, about six years old, he suffers from weak eyes, for which Dr. Smith is attending him. He was dressed in a very tawdry manner, in pink, green, and red cotton, with gold tinsel, and a number of charms hung round his neck.

Wednesday, 10th. We intended leaving to-day, but were prevented by thunder, lightning, and heavy rain. I was not well, and so chilly and cold, that with three or four shawls and cloaks over me I could not get warm. A large packet, evidently containing letters, was brought here. It was, however, for Captain Thomas, to our great disappointment.

Thursday, 11th. A fine day. Just before we started I received a letter from John, which was a great relief to my mind; he finds it impossible to get to Cawnpore, and was going to join the army. He wrote from Kurnaul, dated June 2nd; he says that Brigadier Hallifax died there of fever.

We set off at twelve o'clock in a large boat, and our servants in another of the same size. It is very enjoyable going along in this way without any fatigue. We are going up the stream, and have to track up it. I observed a pretty little girl, of about ten or twelve years of age, pulling the boat in company with one or two men for four hours at a stretch, and she did not seem at all tired; they pull by means of a kind of halter round their shoulders; they are a very fine race of men. There was a lovely sunset, which tinged the distant hills with a fine purple hue, the whole range being beautifully reflected in the river, while beyond, the snowy mountains, with their sharp outlines, formed a dark blue background.

Friday, 12th. Another lovely day. We slept last night in the boat, which continued its progress. At five o'clock we reached the place from whence we started in the boats on our way to Sirinugger; the men told us we could not go nearer to Islamabad by water. H. felt convinced we could, both by the map and by Vigne's account. The people here are such storytellers, you cannot believe what they say. H. made them go back. and we were poking about little streams or nullahs—and getting stuck in the mud—for more than an hour without finding any better way, so we were obliged to return, and by that time it was quite dark, and we had to remain the night in the boat. The next morning I felt very ill, probably from the miasma arising from the river.

We obtained a number of coolies to take our things to the city of Islamabad, about three miles distant. H. got out of the boat and walked there. He soon found that the boat would go up to within a quarter of a mile of the town, so he came back and made the boatmen take us a long way up the stream, had the men put into prison, and has given them no payment. I thought it would have been punishment enough to have omitted giving them any "buckshees h."

We went to a beautiful Baradurree (twelve doors) or Summer house, with water flowing beneath, which we could see through the cracks of the planks. H. paid the boatmen in the evening.

We went into the Maharajah's garden close by—a wretched apology for one; near the entrance are five little knobs, intended for fountains. They throw up water about half a foot high only, and I thought them rather an eyesore than otherwise. There is a kind of house where the Maharajah stays when he comes here, no farmer in England, however small, would think it good enough for himself and family to live in.

Sunday, 14th. H. visited Martund this morning, I was much disappointed at not being able to go, but it would have been too fatiguing. The ruins there are exceedingly ancient, and their origin is unknown. H. made some good photographs.

Monday, 15th. There are several sulphur springs near here. H. had the small tent pitched over one, and I had a very nice bath.

The people here are as dirty as usual. Their dress (for both sexes dress alike) is a kind of bedgown of coarse woollen material, reaching half-way between the knee and ankle, always very dirty, and a plain skull cap on the head. The women sometimes add a dirty piece of cloth thrown over their heads, but it is often very difficult to know a man from a woman.

Tuesday, 16th. We left Islamabad early, I in my janpan. H. has had a dandy made for himself, in which he rode, and the Ayah also had a dandy. We have sent the ponies quite a different way, and shall not see them until we reach Dhurumsala. Our path lay principally among wet rice or paddy fields, which nearly cover the valley, though at one place the whole air was filled with the fragrance of the rose—white, blush, and deep pink. We passed some splendid walnut trees, also wild cherries, unripe, or they would have been very refreshing. We reached Shabad, twelve miles, at 11 o'clock, having, according to our custom, breakfasted half-way. We were caught in a slight storm, and the clouds completely covered and hid from our view the snow-capped mountains before us, and at our side.

Half a dozen or more people came to H. to be cured of different ailments, and he did the best he could for them. We have our tents pitched in a pleasant, shady spot covered with grass. To-morrow, if fine, we go over the Bannihal Pass.

Wednesday, 17th. Set off, after my cup of cocoa (a present from Dr. Clement Smith), a little before five o'clock. We passed through Shabad, a small and rather picturesque village, traversed by a stream, and went along rice fields to Vernag, four miles, where we breakfasted. We went to see the celebrated spring, its waters are received into an immense basin, round which there is a walk, and the whole is surrounded by a low octagonal wall, in which there are twenty-four niches. The water is very clear, and abounds with fish. We were told the fountain was very deep. H. sounded it and found it about sixty feet.

The coolies here are very bad, probably they do not understand how to carry a janpan. Twice they let me fall, and my janpan has become very uncomfortable, having worked itself so crooked that I am quite squeezed and have hardly room to sit.

Directly on leaving Vernag, we began to ascend the Bannihal Pass, it was very steep for three or four miles, at one time winding through a wood of filbert trees, or beneath splendid walnut trees, the ground carpeted with beautiful flowers of every description, and I recognized several choice English flowers.

At 11 o'clock we had reached the top of the hill, and I took my last long look at the "Vale of Kashmir." We then began a steep winding descent over stony ground, quite bare of trees, and very different to the other side of the pass. The sky was cloudy or we should have suffered very much from the heat. We did not reach Dehigol till half past two; we halted several times on the road, but I should think we had been fully six hours in motion. We have put down the distance at thirteen miles, but the hill made it appear much more. Only one English lady, I believe, has travelled here before—Lady Lawrence (Sir Henry's wife). The inhabitants come and look at us with the greatest curiosity, and ask such curious questions.

Thursday, 18th. We rose at four o'clock, and were off by half-past. We went up and down three mountains, and along the sides of them; the road was very steep and dangerous in some parts, and I was in great trepidation. It was a long and tedious march, and when we came to the end, at a place called Butlunder, about ten o'clock, we found no village, and no supplies, we could get no milk, and our servants no attah (flour). To add to our troubles, all the coolies, except twelve, ran off directly they had deposited their loads on the ground, and soon after the remaining twelve disappeared, though we had not paid them. I do not know what we shall do to-morrow, and I am afraid these are only the beginning of our troubles. This place is very hot, surrounded on all sides by high mountains, and we had a very hot march here under a cloudless sky. In the evening, the Sepoy whom the Maharajah sent with us, returned from a fruitless expedition in the neighbourhood, in search of coolies; the inhabitants laugh at Goolab Singh's "permit."

Friday, 19th. We are constrained to remain here whether we will or no. However, I was very glad of the rest, and not to be obliged to get up so early. I went to bed last night dead tired. We have only one fowl, so we kept that for dinner, and made a very good breakfast of eggs and English bacon, strawberry jam, and the usual chupatties. We brought so many tins of preserved provisions with us that we are not likely to starve, unless we have to stay here a week or more. We are quite dependent on these coolies, having sent our ponies another way. This place is terribly hot, at 12 o,clock the thermometer stood at 91 inside our double fly tent under a fine walnut tree.

Saturday, 20th. Still halting; affairs are beginning to look serious. In the morning two of our servants went to a village at a little distance to try and get some milk, eggs, attah, etc., but the inhabitants threatened them with stones, so they were obliged to come away. In the afternoon, six of our servants, armed with sticks, went on a foraging expedition to another village, directly they were observed the people locked up their houses and ran away up the hill, the servants, however, found two old fowls, a kid, and a little attah, which they brought away with them, sending word by any chance passer-by that they would pay for them if anyone would come and receive the money. In the evening, two men ventured down, and we paid them double the proper price, but no entreaties would make them bring us any milk, or indeed give us anything that we could not seize by force. Thermometer 93° in the tent in the shade.

Sunday, 21st June. The Sepoy has not returned, and we appear to be no nearer moving than when we first came here. Four or five servants set off at about six last evening, for a village at some distance. They did not come back all night, and we were beginning to be alarmed at their non-appearance. About 8 o'clock this morning, Mettoo (Kidmutgar) returned, bringing eggs and milk for us, and something for himself. The rest went on to another village. He said the inhabitants ran away as usual, but I suppose they left somebody to receive payment. The flies, fleas, and numerous other biting insects are intolerable here, and the heat very great. The thermometer actually rose to 98° in the tent at the hottest time, about 3 o'clock. This is the season of the rains, and when they come I do not know what we shall do.

In the middle of the day the Sepoy came back, and only brought one little chicken; no coolies; he said he could not get any, and always brings the same news—that the Thanadar (mayor or chief man) has run away, and no coolies to be had. By dint of great exertion, and stopping constantly to rest, I think I might walk two miles a day, and I do not see any other way of getting out of this. Then we must, of course, leave all our luggage behind; the Sepoy was our last hope, and now that is gone. The other servants have not yet returned, and it is now 5 o'clock. We went out in the evening to try and get some milk; we met twelve coolies going empty-handed towards Jummo, and they said they would take some of our things, so I put up the few remaining eatables, with wine, and a plate or two—enough for a couple of days—into one kilter, prepared a petarah (square tin box) for our clothes, one tent was to go, I in my janpan, and H. to walk.

Monday, 22nd. I got up before four and dressed, the servants went to call the coolies but only six came, which would have been of no use, so we let them go away. About 9 o'clock, a number of coolies, upwards of twenty, appeared. We knew we must set off soon notwithstanding the heat, if we intended to go at all, as we could not depend on their remaining, and not changing their minds by the evening, so we had our breakfast and set off, taking only the most necessary things, leaving the Ayah and all the heavy boxes behind, and giving away our bedstead, a table, etc. H. was obliged to walk, but the servants were to try and get some coolies for his dandy.* We proceeded about three miles, stopping very often, as the path was entirely uphill, and exceedingly steep, and H. got very tired. While we were taking a long rest, the dandy with two men came up, and we sent to a village and procured three more men.

We had set off at 11 o'clock, and reached a little town about five miles off, between 5 and 6 in the evening. It was an exceedingly steep hill nearly the whole way, worse even than the Pir Punjal, though we crossed no snow. We had to go over a bridge, ten or twelve feet above the torrent, formed of one flat piece of wood and a small tree by the side, but useless for security, being quite twelve inches apart, and there was no railing or anything to hold on by. H. made a man walk in front of me and I held on by him, but it was much worse to look at H. going over than crossing it myself, it bent with every step. H. was very ill in the evening and night from walking in the sun.

Tuesday, 23rd. Rose at four, and was told the coolies were all ready and waiting, but by the time I was dressed, every one, to the number of about thirty, had run away, up to the top of the hill above us, some 400 feet, and there they sat like monkeys, hiding behind large stones and trees, and no entreaties or persuasions would induce them to come down, not even the promise of extra pay; they afterwards pelted one of the servants with stones. We are, therefore, forced to halt again, having only progressed five miles, after four days halt. It is very strange that these

* Having sustained a severe compound fracture of his right leg some years before, when on duty in Canada, he was not able to walk well.

men should prefer going without their money to finishing the other half of the march, at the end of which they would all have been paid; they appeared anxious to take our loads yesterday; it is past comprehension. The only solution of the enigma that I can think of, is, that they took our loads merely to get us away from the neighbourhood of their villages.

After breakfast, the Ayah turned up, she had been obliged to walk all the way, and I must say did not appear to be at all tired. We had our tent moved a little way up the hill, where we could have more air and partial shade, and the thermometer never rose above 91° in the tent—seven degrees lower than at Butlunder. We sent several of our things on ahead, with two servants, by any stray coolies we could get.

Wednesday, 24th. I thought it so very unlikely we should get any coolies, that I would not get up until they came. About fourteen arrived at 5 o'clock, so we started, merely taking our breakfast things and leaving the remainder—about fourteen loads—to come on as they could. H. shot a Minal pheasant before we set off. We went for the first two miles up the face of the mountain by a zig-zag path, which took us nearly to the summit of this very high mountain, and we looked down on the numerous surrounding peaks. After this we began to descend, and stopped to breakfast at a spring, over which a building has lately been erected. The rest of the march was down hill, with the exception of two or three steep little ascents. The most beautiful ferns grow on the rocky sides of the path, I gathered several different kinds, but they get so withered by the time we reach our camp that I find it difficult, and sometimes impossible, to restore them sufficiently for drying.

This march was a terribly hot one, and we were obliged to stop so often, that it was one o'clock before we reached Nasumon, a small village, surrounded on all sides by high hills, and washed by the muddy waters of the Chinab, at this place a very considerable mountain torrent. We were allowed the use of the Maharajah's house, a very good one as houses go here, though the floor is composed of earth and cow dung However, a tent would have been unbearable in such heat. In the afternoon a terrible hurricane came on.

Thursday, 25th. The Ayah and several of the things did not arrive at all yesterday, no tables, chairs, or bedding. Two bedsteads were lent us, and we happened to have a mattrass, a resai (wadded counterpane) and one sheet, so that we slept as comfortably as the heat, which was excessive would allow. Our pillows were shawls and cloaks. One wants punkahs here, for the thermometer at 5 a.m. was 87° indoors. The Ayah arrived this morning, but eight loads, with one of the Sirdars, are behind, so that we cannot go on. We could get scarcely any milk, just enough at breakfast for two cups, which I made H. have, as I can drink tea without it.

In the evening, a Sepoy came from Sirinuggur, bringing a letter from Colonel Hope Grant. It was dated Alipore, (twelve miles from Delhi), June 5th ; he is in command of the advance force, with Capt. Hamilton as his Brigade-Major. Capt. Anson commands the Regiment, Colonel Yule not having yet arrived.

Friday, 26th. We set off at five. We had to go about a mile, before reaching the rope bridge, over a very dangerous path of loose slates, which kept giving way under the feet of my bearers and rolling down the precipice, the path being in some places only the breadth of a man's foot.

The bridge is composed of twelve thick grass ropes, over this is placed a sort of iron saddle, rope is fastened to this to form a kind of seat for a man, or a load is tied to it, and a thinner rope pulls it backwards and forwards. Each package has to go over separately. It takes a quarter of an hour to fasten the load on, send it to the other side, and receive the empty saddle back, so that half the day was consumed in getting all the things across, and before we made our transit (which I did in the Maharajah's chair, with the Sogdolager, rather frightened, in my lap), it poured with rain. I cannot say that the feeling of being pulled across was at all pleasant, it was effected by a series of jerks. Horses are taken across, I saw several waiting on the other side to be transported over.

We walked to the Baradurree close by, where we remained all day. Our baggage was brought in quite wet.

Saturday, 27th. It rained all night, and we were obliged constantly to move our bed from under the drippings, the roof, unfortunately, not being water tight.

The coolies not having come we could not start until after dinner; we set off about three o'clock, leaving six boxes to come on afterwards, under the care of one of the servants.* We had a very pretty, though disagreeable, march. Our path lay almost the whole way through shrubs and bushes—principally pomegranates, figs, and other fruit trees—which formed a kind of archway through which my janpan had to make its way in the best manner it could. Sometimes the men were obliged to carry it close to the ground to bring it on at all, and with all my care I could not avoid occasionally receiving a severe flick across the face from a branch—lucky for me when it was not of rose bush

* We saw no more of these until the 21st of July, after having quite given them up for lost.

or other prickly shrub, and after a short time, when the rain came on, I had a double shower bath, for the top and curtains of my janpan were continually being dragged off.

The road in some places was very dangerous, and I was obliged to walk. At one place when the path was along a projection of the mountain or rock, the most lovely view burst upon us. We looked down on the winding stream of the Chinab, which here unites the broadness of the river with the rush of the torrent, high mountains rose abruptly on each side of its banks, and a splendid rainbow formed a perfect arch over it, while in the distance, the dim outlines of the further ranges were just visible through the mist, and at intervals the stillness was broken by a loud peal of thunder, which was echoed by every separate range. I never witnessed so grand a scene.

We were obliged to stop about five miles from the place where we intended to halt as it was getting dark, and the rain pouring in torrents. While our tent was being put up we tried to get a little shelter under the only tree we could find. We were very wet, even the mattrass of my janpan was soaked, and when our tent was ready, the ground on which it stood was wet, the carpet and bedding wet, and we had no bedsteads. A number of people came to the tent, notwithstanding the rain, to see "white people," they said, for the first time.

Sunday, 28th. Up at four, and after waiting half an hour for the coolies, we set off, and breakfasted at a village. We found Chinini too far for to-day's march, so stopped at a place called Butot, three miles from it, and pitched our little camp near a grove of fine cedar trees.

A number of women came to look at me, and they brought some apples, apricots, and milk. I gave them some little things, such as needles, sheets of paper, etc., and H. administered medicine and advice to them, and particularly recommended cleanliness, without much hope of its being attended to. They are very fond of having medicine given to them, and often ask for it when in perfect health. H. gave a coolie, who had goitre, some iodine; it is very prevalent here, and appears to affect men and boys as well as women.

The road to this place was so bad, I had to get out and walk several times, or I should rather say, climb, for it was along rock and slate dust, no path, and in some places no footing, and a frightful precipice beneath. One man walked in front of me and another behind, and with a stick in one hand, and clinging to the rock with the other, or holding on by the man when going over the stratum of slate, I managed to get over without accident, and with only one or two slips, and I rather enjoyed the excitement.

We saw two wild goats on this march, the first living things we have seen (with the exception of a few small birds) since we have been in the Hills; we constantly hear the call of the black partridge, but they never show themselves. We passed a very curious Hindoo temple, formed of logs of wood carved with all manner of devices; there were two wooden idols inside, male and female, with their faces all smeared over with ghee (clarified butter).

The wild apricots are ripe, some are a good size, and have a fine flavour, others are small and insipid. The figs are of three kinds, some very large filled with a thick jelly, the middle sized are not generally good, but there is a small kind about as large as a pigeon's egg, which are rather nice. It rained all the afternoon.

Monday, 29th. We halted, to give the baggage behind an opportunity of coming up, but we were disappointed.

In the evening, after a rainy morning, we took a stroll, the view was beautiful, the various tints of the different ranges looked so clear after the rain, and numerous villages surrounded by their cultivated fields, dotted the sides of the hills.

Tuesday, 30th. Woke at half past-three, called for the coolies, had tea—there was only one biscuit remaining. I got up at a quarter to four, and had to wait for the coolies till nearly five, The road was very dangerous in some parts, and the coolies bad, they threw me down three times. On leaving Butot, we went up-hill for about three miles, and came to a fine piece of table land, from which we had a fine view, and a sight of the plains of the Punjab. We reached Chinini at eleven o'clock, having breakfasted as usual, on the way. All our little stock of tea and cocoa is out, the rest being behind, we have only some bottles of essence of coffee, but, as we could get no milk we were obliged to content ourselves with water. The whole town turns out to gaze on us, and our tent is always surrounded by people, who watch our every movement, and are particularly amused by our way of eating dinner, with knives and forks instead of fingers. Thermometer after sunset 82°, yesterday at the same time it was 68°.

[*July*, 1857.]

Wednesday, 1st. H. had a Dhoolie lent him by the Kardar to travel in as far as Ramnuggur. The country on this march was singularly barren, though, perhaps scarcely uninteresting, the mountains are dotted all over with huge stones, the result of some terrible internal convulsion in past ages. We selected one little oasis studded with palmettoes, to halt at for our breakfast, and reached Buttee at three o'olock, a nice halting place, near a sculptured well; a few huts were scattered about at long intervals, otherwise, there was no village. We got a fine large sheep here, for which, however we paid more than we should have done in the plains, and when I wanted a pudding the cook told me it had no suet! We had a tongue dressed, the last of our preserved provisions, with the exception of some tins of soup, sardines, etc.

Thursday, 2nd. After travelling for some time, we arrived at the brow of a hill, and I was pleased with the view of a good sized plain, a relief after so much hill scenery; descended into it, and came to Odinpore, which seems a large town with unusually broad streets. We encamped under a fine tree, a species of fig.

Friday, 3rd. We were up and dressed before the stars had ceased to shine, and were "under weigh" by 4.30. Crossed a deep river by fording, passed close to a fine large fort, and through the town of Jhaghan. Some monkeys came and sat down within a few yards of us, and surveyed us as we passed. We also saw large flocks of goats browsing on the sides of the rocks; their gambols and the fearless way in which they spring over the dangerous ground was interesting to watch. They feed here all day, and are driven into the villages at night. This was a terrible march, very hot, and we were thirteen hours on the road. We descended into Ramnugger by steps cut in the perpendicular rock. We arrived about six, and did not get our dinner till eight o'clock, having breakfasted at half-past seven. Notwithstanding the lateness of the hour, I had my usual bath before dinner, which does more than anything towards taking away fatigue.

Saturday, 4th. We are living in a beautiful Baradurree most elaborately ornamented. We slept in a room upstairs it being cooler; the floor was of white marble, and the ceiling was formed of looking-glass arranged in patterns. H. went to see the Fort this morning, and I was to have gone to the Palace in the evening, but was prevented by a tremendous storm. The Wuzzeer called on H. who gave him one pound of gunpowder, and he sent us some plantains and mangoes, both very good, but the former were the best and largest I have ever seen.

Sunday, 5th. We set off at about five o'clock, and had some rain soon after leaving Ramnugger, and again in the afternoon a storm broke on us at the top of a hill, and I was soon wet through. We did not get to the end of our march till past six, having been again thirteen hours on the road. Nine o'clock came, and still the Khidmutgar with the dinner things, and part of the large tent had not arrived, so we were obliged to go to bed in the small single tent, dinnerless, lying on the ground, with the water running down the sides of the tent, which completely wetted all the bedding; and it continued to rain all night. At eleven o'clock the things came, and by twelve o'clock we managed to get some chupatties made, and a tin of mock turtle soup warmed, but I had been asleep and did not feel inclined to eat, and the Sogdologer even was too tired to help me.

Monday, 6th. Left at 5.30. We came to a beautiful clump of trees at 9 o'clock, where I wanted to wait and have breakfast, (later than we usually have it, and I had had no dinner the day before), but the coolies said there was a nice place beyond, so on we went for nearly a mile when H., thinking the place would not suit, ordered all the things back again. The head man of the place came, and offered H. silver, which of course he merely touched, according to custom.

We reached Mornapore at five. Found out a trick of the coolies; at the end of a march, one of our servants counts the coolies, and we pay them, to-day we happened to count the loads, and found there were several more men than loads, so we paid them accordingly.

Tuesday, 7th. Left early, and marched to Shabad, which we reached about twelve o'clock. We went a mile or so beyond, to the river Rave, near which we had our tents pitched. After dinner, we went on the river on mussucks, which are inflated buffalo skins; on two of these a charpoy was placed, one for each of us, four men paddled us along, each lying across a skin, face downwards, guiding us with one hand, and using a paddle in the other, they used their legs also as paddles, and it had a most singular effect.

Wednesday, 8th. Up at three o'clock, as we had to cross the river; a boat belonging to our Government took us and our baggage over; the mussucks belong to the Maharajah. It was five o'clock before they brought the boat over to our side, by which time it had begun to rain heavily and everything got well soaked in two minutes; I could not keep myself dry in my janpan, though H. had raised the roof of it in the middle to let the rain run off the blanket. At sunrise it cleared, and we had a very hot day.

We stopped at a little bungalow about half way, belonging to some officers of the 4th N.I. We had our dinner, changed coolies, and set off again about six o'clock, reaching Noorpoor at ten; it was said to be six miles but it must have been more. The whole distance from Bisuli to Noorpoor is twelve coss, or about eighteen miles; it was full moon, and much pleasanter travelling then than in the heat of the day, but I was rather nervous—particularly if I happened to be in front—when we met a number of men, fearing that they might be mutinous Sepoys, and would kill us. I made H. load his revolver. We had some coffee, and were in bed by twelve o'clock, having been up for twenty-one hours!

Thursday, 9th. At four this morning we were awakened by a storm; the servants began to make a trench round the tent, but it was too late; lighted a candle, and found the water running through the tent in a stream—it had been pitched in a water course! The Ayah had left all the things on the carpet on the ground, and everything including our bedding (which was on the floor as we had no bedsteads), was completely soaked. I walked about up to my ankles in water, trying to save a few of the things that were uppermost, and then sat on a chair to wait for daylight. By six it had stopped raining, and we found that there was a Dâk Bungalow to which H. took me in my lindsey dressing gown, and wet boots, then he went to learn the news. To our great suprise, Delhi has not fallen, and I was very much grieved to hear that Colonel Yule had been killed on the 21st of June, leading on the Regiment which he was commanding.

This was my brother John's birthday. How little did I think when I rose in the morning, what I should have to go through in the course of this very long day!

Major and Mrs. Wilkie asked us to spend the day with them, and we went there as soon as I could unpack and put on some dry clothing. After breakfast, the man, whom we sent four days ago with a letter to the senior officer at Noorpoor, made his appearance; he had only gone one march a day, and must have missed us while we were resting at the Bungalow half way here. Major Wilkie had sent us a large batch of newspapers, and two letters from the post-office, telling us the dreadful and unexpected news of my dear brother's* death, so long ago as the 8th of June, he was therefore dead when I received his last letter. He was leading a party of the 75th (Queens), in an attack on a twenty-four pounder Battery in front of Budlee-ke-Serai, which they took, but poor John while talking to an officer of the Goorkhas, was struck by a bullet which entered his mouth, passing out at his spine, and of course it killed him instantaneously.

There is a young lady staying here, a Miss Winfield, niece of Major Wilkie, whose step-brother was murdered at Delhi, and she was one of those who managed to escape. Of poor General Barnard's death I also heard, from cholera before Delhi.

A lady (Mrs. Fookes), happened to be going from here to Dhurumsala this afternoon, so it was arranged that I was to go at the same time; then came the parting with my husband, he had to stay till the next morning, having a deep river to cross by daylight; he goes to Jellunder by dhoolie dâk, and thence on to Delhi by mail-cart.

We left at 5 p.m., one of the officers sent a khidmutgar out the first stage to give Mrs. Fookes some tea; we reached the bungalow about eleven o'clock, and the tea was most refreshing; she has a little girl of sixteen months old with her but has just lost her baby boy. We travelled in dhoolies, with twelve bearers, eight at a time, my dhoolie was so large and hung so low, that I was knocked against, and with difficulty dragged over, every projecting stone, which tired and hurt me very much, and I was also too miserable to sleep.

*Captain John Weston Delamain, 56th B.N.I.

I did not reach the Arnolds until one p.m. on the 10th, very much fatigued and so stiff I could hardly walk. The distance from Noorpoor to Dhurumsala is between thirty and forty miles only, but the road is bad and very hilly.

My cousins, the Saunders, are safe at Meerut, Matilda having escaped from Moradabad riding astride on a horse, Charles had a gun pointed at him, but was saved through the intercession of another man. William Ford is also safe after escaping many dangers.

I went to bed dead tired at ten, having had, out of sixty seven hours, only four hours sleep! The 4th N.I. at Noorpoor and Kangra, were quietly disarmed two days after we had passed through the former place, they are believed to be perfectly loyal and so far have behaved well, but it is madness to trust any Regiment. The 46th at Sealkote, loud in their protestations of loyalty, and praying to be led against their mutinous brethren at Delhi, rose on Thursday last, murdered Brigadier Brind and as many Europeans as they could find, and are endeavouring to join the rest of the mutineers at Delhi. The movable column under General Nicholson attacked them, and it is said killed between one and two hundred, but they managed to keep their solitary gun, which was well worked by Brigadier Brind's Khansamah (butler), and retreated across the river.

General Johnstone who was so unfortunate in the Jellundher affair has been upset in a palkee gharie and a good deal injured.

I had a letter from H. from Jellundher, where he arrived after thirty-two hours dâk, and another from Umballah, in which he tells me that Colonel Grant had a horse shot under him in the action of the 9th of July, then I had no letter for three days. I hear there was an engagement on the 14th, but H. could not have been in time for that.

Sunday, 19th. Went to Divine service at Mr. Macleod's large house. Mr. Merk, (a German missionary) from Kangra, did duty and administered the Holy Communion. William Arnold has been very ill for some days.

After church, three envelopes from H. came, one dated 15th from Delhi, another enclosing a letter from my mother acknowledging the receipt of mine, saying John and I had put off coming home till the autumn—oh fatal procrastination!—and one from my darling John written the day before his death.

Monday, 20th. A letter from H., Delhi, 16th, and one from Kurnāl, 14th, which latter must have lost its way! He wants me to send the Syce down to him immediately, and he was off in two hours. Mrs. Rennel Taylor has lent me her second janpan, there are none to be bought here. I have hired four men and am having clothes made for them.

Tuesday, 21st. I was delighted with the sight of our luggage arriving this morning not having seen or heard anything of it since the 26th of last month. I shall now have a decent dress to wear, (I am already in mourning for my husband's mother.)

Wednesday, 22nd. A letter from H. dated 19th, he went to the spot where J. fell, had him exhumed, taken to the burial ground, called up the clergyman at 10.30 p.m., and in presence of two officers of the Rifles, the service was read over his body.

I called on Mrs. Reginald Saunders, she is in great anxiety about her brother (Cautley) who was escaping from his station, Fyzabad, in a boat, with eight others, six are reported killed.

the
vans
just
only
lady
Mrs.
Mrs.

nnel
poys
22nd
lajor
aged.
from
Mrs. Grant, I was very sorry to hear that her sister Mrs. Mordaunt Ricketts had lost her husband, he was murdered at Shahjehanpore.

It was reported long ago, and I am afraid it is true, that Sir Hugh Wheeler and his troops have been all cut up, and the safety of the people at Cawnpore seems very doubtful. It is said they are all massacred, ladies and children amongst the number.

August, 1857.

William Arnold received a letter from Sir John Lawrence informing him that he would not receive his July's pay till October*. August's in December, and September's in January. There was rather an unpleasant paragraph in it to the effect that "Sir J. L. regretted the inconvenience officers may be put to, but they, themselves, must see the necessity of it, for it is best to submit to temporary inconvenience than, for want of funds, to give up the struggle

* He was Director of Public Instruction in the Punjab.

altogether." News has come that the 26th Regiment at Lahore have mutinied, and left the place.

Sunday, 2nd. Authentic accounts have arrived of the massacre at Cawnpore, and of the total destruction of Sir Hugh Wheeler's force. It is said, on his being mortally wounded, his force surrendered to the enemy on condition of their being allowed to go in safety to Allahabad or some other station. They were permitted to get into the boats and then fired upon; one boat got away for ten miles but was pursued, brought back, and all who were not killed on the river were taken to the barracks and there butchered. A few of the names of those murdered are published, and amongst them I see several officers of the 56th. How thankful I feel now that dear John died nobly on the field of battle instead of being miserably butchered with his regiment at Cawnpore.

Monday, 3rd. A short but most severe shock of earthquake. A quantity of snow has fallen on a high mountain near; it is very early in the year for it. In the evening there was a vast bank of fleecy clouds resting on the low hills beneath us, it resembled the sea agitated by a storm; above, the sky was perfectly clear.

Thursday, 6th. There was a dinner party here. Mrs. Edward Paske, Mrs. William Paske, Mrs. Rennel Taylor, and the Saunders' party. H's name has been seen in the *Gazette* as Major in the 2nd Dragoon Guards.

On Friday, 7th, a second daughter was born to the Arnolds. We have just received intelligence of Sir Henry Lawrence's death at Lucknow, a loss that will be deeply felt. A letter from Mrs. Saunders, from Meerut, mentions a Mr. Vibart there, who has lost eight near relations including his father and mother.

sala ;
nner,
other
early
man,
dead.
close
o the

econd
inner
st en-
have
oung-
[illegible] oung-
husband is in a Sikh Infantry Regiment at Kangra.

Monday, 24th. A letter from H. gives an interesting but painful account of the preservation and escape of a Mrs. Leeson, from Delhi. She was a half-caste but the daughter of an officer. When all the European inhabitants were being murdered at the beginning of the outbreak, she was endeavouring to escape. She had her baby in her arms and two other children with her, a boy of four and a girl of three years old. She met some Sepoys who fired at her, and the bullet went through the child in her arms, and wounded her severely in the breast. The child was killed, and she fell to the ground senseless from the effects of her wounds. When she came to herself she found the other two children clinging to her, a sepoy came up, and taking the boy up he cut his throat with his sword, he then took the girl and cut her across the face, just below the nose, and threw her on the body of the mother. After these

* Store-room.

wretches had gone, an old man and his wife brought her to their house, and took care of her. The boy was dead, but the poor little girl lived for six hours. Eventually, an Afghan dressed her up as his wife, got her out of the Gate, and brought her into the camp.

Thursday, 27th. We hear that Lucknow is all right, and General Havelock within ten miles of it.

Friday, 28th. In a letter from H. he tells me he has seen a letter from one of the Cawnpore survivors, it discloses terrible suffering on the part of our people; nearly all of whom either died or were killed. The whole of the Europeans, with the ladies and children, entrenched themselves in the hospital, they were surrounded on all sides, and the enemy soon destroyed and burnt every portion of the building by means of carcases, the ladies then had no place to go to but the trenches, exposed to a burning sun all day. The Nana Sahib (Dundoo Punt), a most desperate villain sent a native woman into the trenches with proposals for a surrender, four officers then went out and were well treated. Boats were got ready, and the party marched out, no sooner were they in the boats than these miscreants opened fire from some masked guns, and they were all destroyed, or brought back to be butchered, except, I believe, four who saved themselves by swimming.

Saturday, 29th. Eddie's sixth birthday—The Sealkote and the Reginald Saunders dined here and in the evening a number of children—nearly all those in the station—came with their Mothers, the verandah was lighted up with three hundred little lamps, and some lanterns of coloured paper and talc which looked very pretty, with plenty of evergreens and flowers; the children, and indeed everyone, seemed much pleased with the entertainment.

Sunday, 30th. We hear that the Simla district is much disturbed, and that an outbreak is expected at Lahore. We are now in the middle of the rains, and scarcely see the sun at all. In the night we had a tremendous storm, and all the doors and windows of my bedroom suddenly burst open.

[*September* 1857.]

Wednesday, 2nd. H's letter was brought in late last night, having been picked up on the road by a Chuprassie. Mrs. Edward Paske has a son born to-day.

Overland mail in, by which I see H's exchange to the 2nd Dragoon Guards is cancelled. The "Extra" says that the Hill station of Murree has been attacked by a number of men, from some adjacent villages, they had, however, been repulsed, and assistance has been sent up from Rawul Pindee.

Monday, 7th. Mr. Merk came over from Kangra, and baptized baby in the drawing room, she is called Frances Egerton, Miss Arnold, myself and Miss Parsons are the godmothers, Mr. Egerton of Lahore, godfather. Afterwards there was a party at luncheon, or early dinner.

Friday, 11th. A letter from H.—short and almost illegible—saying he had been seized with cholera the morning before, but he was then, he thought, out of danger.

The *Lahore Chronicle* gives a distressing account of the defence and abandonment of the fort at Futteghur, the Europeans left in boats, and floated down the river towards Cawnpore, but were seized by the Nana Sahib, and after a few days, butchered in the Assembly Rooms. Colonel

Goldie* and his two daughters were among the number. One daughter was seized by the mob, and given over to the Nawab, what her fate was, and that of two other young ladies with her, is not known.

The 28th N.I., which was stationed at Umballah when we first went there, mutinied at Shajehanpore, and murdered several people; others—among them the Lysachts—escaped, and travelled fifty miles towards Lucknow, but were there met by another mutinous regiment, and all killed. I constantly hear of acquaintances who have been murdered in this terrible mutiny. There is a list published of the officers who have been massacred, or killed in defending their forts or stations, the number already known is two hundred, then there are the women and children, and persons belonging to the uncovenanted service. Those who have fallen in battle and died of natural causes before Delhi number thirty six.

Saturday, 12th. A letter from H., thank God he is better though very weak.

Monday 14th. A dinner party—Colonel and Mrs. Abbott, Mrs. Rennel Taylor, Mrs. R. Saunders, Miss Cautley, and Mr. E. Paske.

Tuesday, 15th. In H's letter he tells me that the tent I sent with Isri, which he wanted so much, has been kept at Umballah by Mr. Parker, notwithstanding our instructions to him to send it on as quickly as possible; also the Banghy parcel† I sent to Delhi with so many valuable little things in it nearly a month ago has not arrived so I am afraid it is lost.

Wednesday, 16th. This morning we heard that Delhi had fallen, that the attack commenced at 3 a.m. of the 14th, and was over at 8 a.m. Shortly afterwards other messages

* His son is a cornet in the 9th Lancers.
† Similar to our parcel post.

came in with accounts that fighting was still going on; one of the columns making very slow progress, however we are in the city.

Received a letter from H. dated 13th, he expected the attack would take place the next day, our batteries having done great execution on the walls; he went to the front and got to within three hundred yards of the city walls, but the musketry was so severe it was impossible to go on. Dr. Sinclair Smith of the 9th went just after H. when a random shot—a twenty-four pounder—killed his horse and he had a very narrow escape. We dined early at the Reginald Saunders', to celebrate Flory Taylor's second birthday. We were all in a state of great excitement, news constantly coming in; we hear that General Nicholson, who commands one of the columns of attack is dangerously wounded, but we must wait till to-morrow before the list of killed and wounded will arrive. What a time of anxiety!

Thursday, 17th. *Lahore Extra* came early this morning with a list of three officers killed, and a great number wounded. Fighting still going on, on the morning of the 15th, and we only appear to have won about a quarter of the city. I suppose there will be no time to write letters, so I must not expect any.

Friday, 18th. An annular eclipse of the sun, it began about 8.15 a.m. and lasted some two hours; clouds came up and hid the sun for some time, but we got a very good view of it just at the full, it was a most interesting sight. The telegraph from Delhi good on the whole, but the progress is slow, news up to the morning of the 16th. I scarcely expected it, but got a letter from H., dated Kashmir Gate Sept. 15th, 12.30 p.m., he was writing in a house which they were defending against the enemy, few Sepoys had been killed as yet, forty of the 9th Lancers were wounded, six of them very badly, no officers hit. The Saunders' party and Dr. Trevor Lawrence drank tea here, and we played *vingt-et-un* as Willie said, to drive away thought.

Saturday 19th. News by *Lahore Extra* only up to the evening of the 16th, the magazine which we took with little loss in the morning had been attacked by the enemy who were however repulsed, but with the loss of several killed and wounded on our side. Another letter from H. dated 16th, none of the 9th Lancer officers touched, but they had eight horses hit, Mr. Hamilton's nice brown charger being killed by a grape shot.

Sunday, 20th. On my way to church I received my letter, we are gaining ground at Delhi, slowly but surely.

Monday, 21st. My letter from Delhi of the 18th does not give quite such good accounts, no progress made since H. last wrote; we failed in an attack on the Lahore Gate, the——th could not be got to advance. H. says sickness increases (the *Extra* says not) that there are 3,000 sick, and that 200 go into hospital every day, and in fact we have too few men.

Tuesday, 22nd. Heard the welcome intelligence of the total occupation of Delhi, by our troops.

[*October*, 1857.]

From the 22nd of September to the 22nd of this month I have been very ill indeed. After about a fortnight Dr. Lawrence who was attending me wished for another opinion and Dr. Williams was sent for from Kangra, a station about twelve miles distant. At one time I was so ill I scarcely expected or wished to recover, however, about the 15th I began to get better and a few days after was carried to a sofa in the next room, but I am so exceedingly weak I can neither walk nor stand.

H. is commanding the Cavalry Brigade of Colonel Greathed's Column, which is going down country to clear the disturbed districts. On the 27th of September he was ordered to destroy a village, which he did by burning it, he found a number of ladies' bonnets, dresses, shoes, etc., and a packet of letters.

In an affair on the 28th of September at Bolundshur, we lost a good many, killed and wounded, among the latter was Mr. Sarel, shot through the left arm, and four fingers of his right hand had to be amputated. Young Blair had the head of the bone of his shoulder blade amputated, and will it is feared lose the use of his left arm; he rode at a Sowar and thrust his lance through his body, but the Sowar managed to cut through Blair's left shoulder before he died. Captain Drysdale who was commanding the 9th, had his horse shot while charging through the town, and broke his collar bone, Mr. Thonger was also wounded, and Mr. Edgeworth of the 8th, wounded in the arm.

The villagers in that part are against us, and cut up any stragglers, concealing themselves in the Khets* when the Column is passing.

The Fort at Malyghur was blown up; a dreadful accident happened there: Holmes the Engineer who had distinguished himself so much before Delhi, and was to have received the Victoria Cross, by some mismanagement, blew himself up with the fort, he was killed;—and another European had both his legs broken.

In another letter, H. says he heard there was an English

* High crops.

lady in a village near. He sent three hundred cavalry and they brought her into camp, she turned out to be a half caste girl, about sixteen years old—a Sowar had taken her away, and she said she liked him, and did not wish to leave him.

I read in the *Lahore Chronicle* after a Cavalry affair of Colonel Greathed's Column "the Officer in command of the Cavalry deserves great credit for the noble manner in which he handled his Brigade," etc.

In the early part of October we heard that Lucknow had been relieved by Sir James Outram and General Havelock, and that half the city had been taken. M. Saunders has joined her husband at Delhi, and is actually living in the Palace.

I had such an interesting letter from H., with an account of the battle of Agra, on the 10th of October. When the moveable column was near Akbarpore, some 42 miles from Agra, they received urgent letters from Colonel Frazer (Chief Commissioner) requesting the Cavalry and Artillery to come on to Agra by forced marches. H. was off immediately, marched 34 miles that night and the next day, and they reached the encamping ground at Agra at 9 o'clock on the morning of the following day. H., and nearly all the officers, went into the fort to breakfast: he was just on the point of leaving, and our Bombay cart was waiting to take him back, when a report came from camp that the enemy was upon them. H. rushed out of the fort seized upon a Buggy and with Colonel Cotton drove off to camp, two miles distant, found Captain Fawcett in command of the 9th, saw one of our Sikh regiments formed into a square, and the enemy's cavalry coming up at a gallop; they took a gun and killed the men who were working it, but [did not keep it long, for H. was on them with the Lancers, and they broke and fled. The Infantry soon after came out of the fort, and a regular advance was made. After we had taken two large guns the enemy began to retreat. The order was then given for a pursuit, with the whole of the Cavalry. H. left two squadrons of Lancers to protect the camp, and then pursued the flying foe for ten miles, till they came to a river, when they gave the fugitives the last shot. We captured guns, baggage, and an enormous amount of plunder. Poor Captain French* was killed, and H. fears Mr. Jones* is mortally wounded. Mrs. Reginald Saunders and Miss Cautley have at length received authentic accounts of their brother's death: he belonged to the 22nd N.I., and escaped from Fyzabad with the Serjeant-Major of another Regiment; they were attacked by villagers, and were making their escape, when young Cautley it is supposed, was seized with cramp, and was unable to proceed; he was forced to sit down and await his pursuers; the other man ran on, and presently, looking back, he saw the villagers hacking him in pieces.

Mrs. William Paske heard for the first time of the murder of her brother, Mr. Smalley, from a letter received from her mother in England. Mrs. Hall's father, Colonel Goldney of Fyzabad was also murdered, but she refuses to believe it, and will not put on mourning, though everyone else is convinced of the truth of it.

Thursday, 22nd. William Arnold, who has been very ill, but is now much better, started for Lahore to-day. Fanny with baby and Miss Cautley march with him as far as Hooshiapore. Miss Parsons (the governess), the three children and myself, are left in charge of the house. I have

* Both 9th Lancer Officers. Lt. Alfred Stowell Jones eventually recovered with the loss of an eye, and covered with scars. He had already won the Victoria Cross, for some act of gallantry.

received several English letters dated May 3rd, I cannot think where they have been all this time!

Saturday, 31st. A letter from H., dated Oct. 23rd Kanoj, giving me an account of his successful affair there. He crossed the river, took all the enemy's guns, killed 200, and drove many into the Ganges, where they were drowned. A gallop of 14 miles, after a march of 24 that day, and 40 the day before had tired him, but they were going 24 more that night, as they had heard bad news from Lucknow. General Havelock is besieged in the Residency and has only provisions, it is said, to last till the 10th.

I went out in the janpan for the first time for nearly six weeks, but the exertion was too much for me, and I fainted—the janpan was brought into the room, and I was wheeled up to it in a chair that has castors.

[*November* 1857.]

Monday, 2nd. We hear that a conspiracy to seize the fort at Bombay, and murder all the Christians, has been discovered in time to prevent it from being carried out.

Thursday, 5th. Miss Parsons and the children went down the hill to spend the evening at Mrs. Younghusband's, to celebrate the first birthday of Mrs. Hughes' little boy. Between forty and fifty Europeans have arrived at Kangra so the fort there will be well guarded now.

Previous to my illness, I was accustomed every night before going to bed, to put all my little valuables together in a bag by my bedside, in case of a midnight alarm, afterwards such a precaution would have been useless, as I was so weakened, I could not have run a yard to save my life.

Saturday, 7th. The third anniversary of our leaving

England. I see by the English papers that Major Rose is promoted to a Lt. Colonelcy in the 17th Dragoon Guards, so H. is now Senior Major, which is the best thing that could happen to him, for if all goes well we shall be able to remain with the regiment in England, and I hope we may never come to this country again.

Wednesday, 11th. Miss Parsons and the children started early this morning to meet their mother at Kangra. Miss Cautley rode on, and came to sleep here that I might not be alone in the house. They all returned the next day.

The country is in a most disturbed state, Mr. Neville, an officer of the 81st Queens, who was proceeding down one of the rivers in the Goojaira district, on his way to England, has just been murdered. His was a particularly sad case, for his intended bride was on her way out to him, and the first thing she heard on reaching Bombay, was of his death.

Wednesday, 18th. Mrs. Farrington had a son this morning.

We went down in our janpan, to look at the church, the side walls are nearly up, and the framework of the east window is being put in.

I am at last able to walk a little, but feel very much as if my legs did not belong to me, and walk in a very staggering way. On Sunday 22nd, I went to Divine Service (of course in my janpan) at Mr. Macleod's bungalow, he is up here now and read the service—I had greatly overrated my strength, and though I sat down the whole time, I was miserably tired on reaching home.

Monday, 23rd. Mrs. Younghusband and Mrs. Hughes, (who was I believe a Miss Buller, of Downes) with their respective babies, spent the day here. Mrs. Hughes draws very well, and has sent some sketches to the Illustrated London News.

Wednesday, 25th. No tidings from Lucknow, very anxious. Two Cossids (messengers) I hear have been seized on their way from Cawnpore to Agra, with despatches.

Twenty-three persons, all of one family, have their names recorded in one paper, as having been massacred at Delhi.

Friday, 27th. After eight days' anxiety, a letter came this morning from H.—if indeed it may be called a letter, its length being 3 inches, and its breadth ¾ of an inch. He was that day (15th Nov.) put into command of the regiment again. Colonel Little who has just joined is made Brigadier, and Colonel Grant the General Commanding.

H. has not received a single line from me for more than three weeks. If there is no post between Cawnpore and Lucknow, surely letters might be sent on with the troops, who are so constantly moving about.

The hills all about Dhurumsala which are very little higher than this are white with snow, and it is bitterly cold

Sunday, 29th. The *Moffussilite* tells of an engagement and of the relief of Lucknow on the 16th, five officers are killed and thirty wounded.

[*December*, 1857.]

Sunday, 6th. Went to Mr. Macleod's bungalow for service in the morning, and down the hill to the Kutcherry (police office), in the evening.

Friday 11th. My birthday—hoped for a letter from H. but was disappointed.

Wednesday, 15th. A violent shock of earthquake occurred at about seven in the morning—it woke me out of my sleep and continued so long that I got up and went out of my room into another before it ceased. This is the second shock I have felt here, and the most severe.

Lady Lawrence is going to England with her two children, and Sir John accompanies her as far as Moultan. She has sent Flory a very pretty little pony.

Saturday, 18th. News came this morning from Colonel Seaton's camp of a Cavalry and Artillery affair with the Khasgunge rebels. The Carabineers lost three officers, Wardlow, Hudson, and Vyse. Captain Head of the 9th, doing duty with them, was severely wounded. We appear to have suffered the greatest loss, ours being sixty, while the enemy's was apparently only fifty men.

Monday, 20th. A *Lahore Extra* at last brings some intelligence of what is going on down country, of the defeat of the Gwalior Contingent, without giving, however, many particulars. A private letter published in it speaks casually of the great loss we have experienced in the death of Sir Henry Havelock, when, where and how it took place, we do not know, this is the first and only intimation we have had of it, the official communication of that as well as of every other occurence lately having been cut off.

Thursday, 24th. It is just four weeks since I last heard from H., this morning the eagerly expected atom of a note was put into my hands, it was dated Cawnpore, December 14th, he had not heard from me for nearly six weeks* when I told him I was better, but not strong enough to stand or walk, he wishes me if I am able to travel, to proceed at once to Umballah, and join him if possible at Cawnpore. He was not at all well, and the doctor tells him he ought to go on sick-leave, he feels the effect of his attack of cholera. He thinks there will be little more fighting. Fifteen guns

* He was two months without a single letter from me, although I wrote almost every day, when well enough.

were taken near Cawnpore; he with the Cavalry killed 90 men, without any loss on our side, they made no resistance and are evidently losing heart. H. wishes me to take a European servant with me, if I cannot travel with a lady, but there is neither one nor the other available here.

We had a gay party this evening; as many people as Dhurumsala afforded assembled here, a brilliantly lighted Christmas tree looked pretty, and was quite a novelty, everyone had a present off it, mine was a sketch book. Christmas Day brought me another but earlier letter from H., it was enclosed in an envelope by some one at Agra, it told me about Wyndham's disastrous battle at Cawnpore.

The Taylors and Saunders dined here. Dr. Lawrence had gone to Noorpoor, to stay with Major Wilkie, to whose regiment he belongs.

Saturday, 26th. Busy packing, but I am not equal to much fatigue yet. I sent off my Khidmutgar and another servant with two mules, and a coolie load, having given away all that was not absolutely necessary except H's photographic things. I gave Eddie my nice white pony, Crab; his mother my side-saddle, and promised to send her our lamp from Umballah, a thing she was much in want of.

We all dined at the Reginald Saunders', as I should be away before New Year's Day. The drawing room chimney caught fire while we were there, we went outside to watch it, it burnt very fiercely; some men were sent to the top to pour down water, and they soon put it out. We were obliged to remain the rest of the evening without fire, and we felt the cold very much.

Sunday, 27th. We all attended service at Major Rennel Taylor's.

Monday, 28th. I left this morning after a very early breakfast. Fanny (Mrs. Arnold) is very unwell indeed* I could not help feeling very sorry to part with them all and leave Rydal Lodge after a residence there of five months and a half. Little Eddie offered me his greatest treasure, a small gun, and little Florrie was most anxious for me to take her pet plaything.

I left in a dhoolie with eight bearers, my Ayah in another, and four Bhangy berdars (bearers) to carry my light luggage, and so I began my solitary journey with a very distant prospect of joining my husband.

After a journey of three hours and a half over hills, I came to Kangra and dined with Mr. and Mrs. Merk—he is a missionary. At four, I again resumed my journey, and reached Purwain Dâk bungalow at 3 o'clock on Tuesday morning. I feel rather courageous at beginning a long journey in such times as these, for the first time alone; but I cannot help sometimes thinking of the horrors that have been enacted lately, and when I am put down in a native village with at least a hundred men standing round my dhoolie, and not a European within twenty or thirty miles, I feel there would be nothing to prevent them from attacking me if they wished it, but, somehow, I did not feel afraid.

On Tuesday evening I set off for Hooshiapore, where I arrived at such an early hour in the morning, that I had my dhoolie put down in the verandah of the Dâk bungalow until 7 o'clock, then I went to Capt. and Mrs. Paske's and found the latter suffering from neuralgia, so she did not appear till the afternoon. Capt. Paske took me for a nice drive in his carriage and pair, such a treat after those disagreable janpans. Just before dinner I discovered, to my surprise, that my dâk was not laid through Jullunder, but a

*She died the March following, and her husband April 1859.

more direct, though less frequented road to Loodiana. This was a great disappointment as I had directed all my letters to be sent to the former place, and Mrs. Farringdon had been asked to receive me there; however, there was nothing for it but to proceed the way my dâk was laid. I was, however, persuaded to remain the night, that Capt Paske might send out Sowars to be ready for me at all the stages, for there were none out on that road. He also sent off an express to Jullunder to have my letters forwarded at once to Loodiana where he said they would arrive as soon as I.

Thursday, 31st. I left Hooshiapore after an early breakfast. Twelve hours dâk brought me to Loodiana by 9 o'clock in the evening. I got some tea and went to bed. I had been provided with some very nice sandwiches and plenty of fruit. I was to have heard at Jullunder from Fanny Arnold whether Mr. Elliott, to whom she had written, could receive me here, as she was so averse to my staying at the Dâk bungalow alone, however, as I had missed my letters and from my change of plan it was evening instead of morning when I arrived, I thought it best to go to the Dâk bungalow.

[*January*, 1858.]

Friday, 1st. I sent Mr. Elliott a packet of books from Willie Arnold, and he came immediately to see me. He had sent people to wait for me at the bridge in order to direct me to his house where there was a room prepared, and he wanted to drive me there at once, but as I wished to leave at about 1 or 2 o'clock I declined his kind offer. He sent me some delicious grapes and oranges, and promised to provide Sowars to see me safe to Umballah. Just as I was leaving I received my packet of letters.

I reached the Dâk bungalow at Khana-ka-Serai at 10 o'clock in the evening; there was nothing to be got here. I ordered some tea which I always carry with me, but the water was bad, this with a slice of very dry bread I had brought with me formed my evening meal, and I cannot say I enjoyed it.

Saturday, 2nd. Up at five, and after a breakfast of tea and bread was off before the stars had ceased to shine. Arrived at Umballah at 6 p.m. in time for dinner. I am staying with Mrs. Anson and Mrs. Bell-Martin, the latter has a fine little girl of five months old—she herself being only seventeen years and a half old—Mrs. Anson's youngest is a splendid boy about three months old the elder children have all got the whooping cough.

Umballah does not appear much changed but it seems strange living in the Artillery, instead of the Lancer lines.

Sunday, 3rd. We went to church in a carriage belonging to the Rajah of Puttiala, who is very kind in lending them for the use of the ladies,—horses, coachman, and all free of expense. The church is surrounded by fortifications bristling with canon and is garrisoned by soldiers. Carriages cannot come inside the fortifications, and it was almost more than I could do to walk to the church door, I am still so weak.

Monday, 4th. I have an immense deal to do, having to collect all our things, furniture, etc., and send them to be sold. All our things are so dispersed that it is almost impossible to manage without a carriage and servants at my command. I do not even know where to look for them. At last I got to the Mess Go-down and ordered some boxes to be sent to Mrs. Anson's for me to pack. I found much furniture and crockery belonging to us in the Mess room

Wednesday, 6th. I called on Mrs. Hope Grant, she has been very ill, but is better; she is ordered home and goes I believe by Bombay, with her widowed sister, Mrs. Ricketts.

Thursday, 7th. I lunched with Mrs. Fooks, she took me in her carriage to the Mess house, and I opened some boxes, but the Moderator lamp I wanted to send to Dhurumsala could not be found anywhere. All our things are in great disorder and many quite spoilt. H. on his way to Delhi took his best clothes out of the drawers and threw them into a stable chest, his dress waistcoat was completely eaten up by insects, also some new waistcoats and overalls, of boots nothing remained but the soles, and his dress, and undress shakos—ten guinea affairs—had been converted into nests where several families of mice had been born and reared!

Mrs. Anson told me H. has only got six weeks' leave and in his letters he says he is better and will most probably not go to England, but will be able to see me off from Calcutta.

Saturday, 9th. I received a short letter from H., saying he is very unwell indeed, and that if I do not join him very soon he will be obliged to go without me; he has had no letters though I have written every day, and he does not know whether I have left Dhurumsala or not.

I started from Umballah about 4 o'clock in a dhoolie, and my Khidmutgar on a pony—my Ayah utterly refused to go down country,—Mr. Barnes, the Commissioner, sent a mounted Sowar with me, but when I came to the end of the first stage (about 11 or 12 miles) he went away and no other came, my change of bearers also was not there; the old ones stayed by me because I would not give them their "bucksheesh" till the relief came, and I thought I should never get on. It does not do with natives to take things too easily, so I made a great fuss, sent one off to look for the Sowar, and another for the bearers, and at the end of three quarters of an hour the coolies arrived but no Sowar, and then the "tattoo wallah"* refused to go on. I could wait no longer and proceeded alone, leaving my servant to do the best he could; after I had gone a few miles he overtook me on the pony, having made some arrangement with the man.

Thirty-five miles from Umballah the road becomes good and at 12 o'clock at night I exchanged my dhoolie for a carriage with my man on the box, in order to go by horse dâk the rest of the way to Delhi, where I arrived, without stopping—except to change horses—at half past 3 on Sunday afternoon. I went straight to Charles and Matilda Saunders at the Palace. William Ford was there and Mr. Charles Raikes and his family.

Monday, 11th. Before leaving I was anxious to see my dear brother's grave; an elephant was the only available mode, and I went on it with Matilda and Mrs. George Campbell. I was, however, quite ill and knocked up with the exertion, and obliged to rest before I could start for Meerut, which I did after a late breakfast, the direct road to Agra being considered unsafe.

The horses here are very bad, I was delayed a whole hour at one chokee by a horse, the only one remaining, which would not allow himself to be put into the shafts, and I fully expected to be obliged to pass the night on the road; however, at last the men managed to harness him by tying ropes to his heels and forcibly keeping them down, and when once regularly in he never thought of continuing to kick, but went on quite well at full gallop.

The iron suspension bridge over the river seems in good

* Man in charge of the tattoo or pony.

order, the rebels I suppose found it too useful to be destroyed.

I reached the Dâk Bungalow at Meerut late in the evening, it looked so solitary and dismal, while some large fires I saw in the distance made me think of burning bungalows, and a great noise and "tom tomming" in the Bazaar did not tend to make me feel more comfortable quite alone in this place, where the first horrors of the mutiny were enacted.

Tuesday, 12th. Mr. Raikes, an old civilian, called for me at 9 this morning, we were to travel to Agra in company and we kept our carriages as near together as possible. The only mishap we had was when we were going along the road full gallop (dâk horses when they go at all generally travel at that pace the whole stage of six miles) something frightened my horse, he turned and ran down the embankment at the side of the road, fortunately it was not very steep and the carriage did not upset. I got out and walked along the road a short distance while the carriage was being hoisted up the bank again, and we were told that the rebels were in great force just the other side of the river which is very near. We passed through Bolundshur and in the evening stopped near a village, sent and had a goat milked and our servants boiled the kettle for tea which we much enjoyed. I wrote a letter to H. in the carriage and posted it as we passed through Alighur, besides sending one from Meerut, so I hope that one of the many may chance to reach him.

Wednesday, 13th. Arrived at Agra about six in the morning; we had to wait sometime outside the town till the gates were open. I had intended to try and find out Lady Outram but the first thing I heard was that she had gone to her son at Alighur

The Dâk Bungalow I knew was burnt down and I did not know what to do till Mr. Raikes told me there was an hotel, when, wishing him good-bye, I drove there calling at the Post Office on my way to find there were no letters for me.

On arriving at the hotel the man said his house was full, but he pointed to a kind of stable or out-house, divided into rooms by straw partitions, very dark and dismal, I did not look at all pleased with the accomodation, and he then said he had a room engaged but not yet occupied which I could have until it was claimed. I got out of my carriage and was somewhat surprised to see that it was perfectly bare and unfurnished, however they fetched me a chair and presently a cup of tea, and a footstool to keep my feet off the cold stone (or chunam); and, after they had brought a table, two chairs, an old-fashioned sofa very hard and uncomfortable, and a somewhat dirty carpet, the room began to wear rather a more comfortable aspect. An arched doorway led into a slip of a room in which a bed was put and after a great deal of search an old curtain was found to separate the two rooms. Almost before this was completed Mr. Raikes came to look after me, he could give me no hope of getting on to Cawnpore. He was going at once to join the Commander-in-Chief's camp and hoped to be able to rescue his little grand-daughter from the hands of the mutineers, he however, here learnt of her death. His poor daughter and her husband (Mr. and Mrs. Christian) and baby had been murdered at Seetapore; the little girl had been spared but she at length died of exposure and the hardships she had to undergo.

I was very unwell again and for two days was entirely confined to my bed and could eat nothing.

Few people have yet ventured to leave the fort, and had they wished to do so they would have found it difficult, as there are hardly any houses left standing, only one or two close to the fort having escaped burning and destruction.

The owner of the hotel only left it two days before I arrived. When we passed up the country in 1855 they had a very good hotel, but of course on the breaking out of the mutiny, they in common with everyone else had to take refuge in the fort, and abandon all their things; their principal bungalow was burnt.

Friday, 15th. I have at last received three letters from H., one re-directed three times from Dhurumsala, another twice from Umballah, the third was dated Cawnpore, January 11th, telling me if I had reached Agra, to go at once to Colonel Frazer and ask for an escort. I know it is useless as he has told me through his wife, who called here, that he cannot give me one. However, I wrote to him, and his answer was, that he had not a single available guard, and it was quite unsafe to go without one; that the Commander-in-Chief had given orders for all ladies desirous of going down country to assemble here on the 12th of next month, and he is afraid there will not be an opportunity sooner—nearly a month! How can I wait all that time?

A convoy left yesterday morning to take supplies to the Commander-in-chief but it returned after going a few miles, it was said on account of the disturbed state of the roads.

Mr. and Mrs. N. Noble called this morning, having heard my name mentioned. They have a very pretty little girl of a year old. Mrs. Innes also paid me a visit, she was a stranger to me, but sister to Major Macpherson, the Resident of Gwalior, who was so kind to us, and with whom we stayed for several days on our march from Bombay to

Umballah. She was staying with him at the breaking out of the mutiny, having left her husband in Lucknow to pay her brother, as she thought, a short visit. They both escaped in a carriage to Agra, and Scindia has taken care of their things. They had not been long at Agra before the outbreak occurred there, when they had to make another flight into the fort. Poor Mrs. Innes of course did not hear from her husband for several months, and knew not until a very short time ago if he were alive or dead. She took me for a drive in the evening, and I dined with them; they have left the fort since I arrived here and are living in tents. I never beheld such a scene of desolation as met my eyes during the drive; the cantonments are a heap of ruins; on each side as you drive along you see nothing but burnt and roofless bungalows. I imagine only a part will be restored as the seat of Government is to be transferred to Allahabad.

I spent the whole of Saturday at Major Macpherson's. Mrs. Innes was very busy making milk punch, to do the duty of wine which is a very scarce commodity.

Sunday, 17th. This is one of the anniversaries of our wedding day, and a dismal one it was, I did not leave my little room or see a single person, and did not even get a letter from H. to cheer me. Service is only held in the fort, and carriages are not allowed inside.

Monday, 18th I spent the day at Colonel* and Mrs. Frazer's, he is the "burra Sahib" here and has just got into a nice house. They have a very delicate young man, a Mr. Williams living with them, who lost a leg in the battle of Agra on the 5th of July.

Tuesday, 19th. I spent at Major Macpherson's, and saw some very good photographs of Delhi and Agra by

* He died a few months later.

Mr. Boldero of the Civil Service—Mrs. Innes sketches well in water colours.

Wednesday, 20th. I received two letters from H. yesterday, one dated Nov. 26th! and one to-day of the 18th inst., in this he tells me he leaves Cawnpore for Allahabad as I wished, and told him to do if it was at all necessary, particularly as I saw no hope of being able to leave this for a long time. However, on Monday I had some slight hope, which to-day is confirmed and I trust to be able to leave Agra on the 22nd, a few ladies who are ready being allowed to go with some guns and ammunition for the Commander-in-Chief. We are to have tents allowed us, one of which I am to share with Mrs. Prendergast a young widow with two children, she lost her husband—a Major in the Bengal army—in July last, from cholera.

Thursday, 21st. Mrs. Simpson, an Umballah friend, sent a tonjon for me, and I spent the day with her and her cousins, Mr. and Mrs. Gilbert, in the fort. Poor Mrs. Simpson, her story is very sad: her husband who was Brigade-Major at Umballah went with the army to Delhi, while there he had a very severe attack of cholera, which obliged him to get leave and he joined his wife at Simla for a month. He then returned to Delhi, which in the meantime was in our possession. Finding things tolerably quiet he wrote to his wife to join him. On her approaching Delhi some troopers came out to meet her; she was rather surprised at not seeing her husband, but they told her he was in Delhi. She was taken to some friend's house, and there learned she was a widow. Her husband had walked out of a window the night before in his sleep, and falling from a height was killed on the spot. She had no idea of the habit, which he had but lately acquired, of walking in his sleep. She has one little boy about two years old. She is now living with her cousin, Mrs. Gilbert who had a narrow escape from Gwalior, her baby, a fine, fat little child was born during the flight, on the banks of the Chumbul. Captain Gilbert was away on duty at the time or would probably have been killed, as all officers were if discovered, although in this case they spared the ladies.

I went yesterday over the fort with Mrs. Innes, she walked while I went in a tonjon (a kind of Sedan chair without a head). There are double gates on all sides and the sentinels never open one till the other is closed. To-night I was a few minutes late in leaving the fort, and the drawbridge had to be lowered on purpose for me.

Friday, 22nd. The camp left Agra to-day; the first march everything is in disorder, and there will be a halt to-morrow to set everything right, we are therefore advised not to join until the next day. I spent the afternoon and evening with Major Macpherson and Mrs. Innes, the latter was rather inclined to accompany the Column, but decided at last to remain and wait for another opportunity.

Saturday, January 23rd. My heavy luggage fortunately arrived yesterday by bullock train from Umballah, just in time to send off in a cart last night with my servants. Colonel Riddell paid me an early visit, having only just heard of my being here. After a cup of tea, I went in a tonjon to take a late breakfast with Mrs. Gilbert and Mrs. Simpson, so as to be in readiness to start from the fort with Lady Outram who has kindly offered to take me the first stage in her carriage, hired for the occasion. We started about 2 o'clock—Lady Outram, her son Frank and I—the wind was blowing in that disagreeable way which raises the dust in clouds, and we had a most uncomfortable drive. A change of horses, however quickly brought us into camp, where we had much difficulty in finding our way amidst the confusion of camels, horses, bullocks, carts, tents, etc., at last we found Lady Outram's "houses," enjoyed a comfortable dinner, and, after some pressing I accepted her kind offer of living with them. Though personally a stranger to her, our respective families have been intimate for years.

About 9 p.m. Major Macpherson arrived bringing Mrs. Innes who had that morning received a letter, which caused her to change her mind about coming. She must have been most expeditious in her arrangements, packing, preparing a tent, getting servants and necessaries for a long march, however, she had her brother to help her. Of course none of her things arrived that night, and she shared my bedding and one of Lady Outram's three tents with me. Sentinels were posted all round close to our tent doors and we were in regular camp order.

Sunday. 24th. The bugle sounded at two o'clock, and we had to be up and dressed early so that the tents might be struck and packed. Tea and biscuits were served in Lady Outram's large tent. The night was pitch dark, and intensely cold with that same disagreeable dusty wind, we were not properly provided with lanterns, and the candles would not keep alight even inside the tent. Mrs. Innes was to share Lady Outram's bullock gharie, and as the carriage H. is sending me from Cawnpore has not yet arrived I was obliged to put up with a Government dhoolie (glad enough however to get anything), and though it was not time to be moving off, yet as the tents were all being taken down I had to retire to my dhoolie, and the rest to their respective conveyances. Mine is a kind of bedstead slung on a pole hanging close to the ground, in the most convenient situation to catch all the dust, with a curtain on each side which never would keep down.

We did not begin our march till about an hour before day-break; I soon got separated from my party, and I could not make my bearers understand anything I wanted (being natives of a different part of the country they did not understand my Hindustanee, nor I theirs), they entangled me in the heavy guns, the orderly officers and sergeants thinking of course that I was a sick or wounded soldier ordered the bearers first here, then there, and scolded them for being out of their line and order, and I did not know what to do or where to go till at last Mr. Outram found me and took me to join the rest of the party.

It was late before we got to our camping ground, and I was one mass of dust and dirt; then the tents could not be pitched before the ground had been marked out, so it was nearly 2 o'clock before we could get our much needed bath and breakfast.

There are about ten ladies in the Column—Lady Outram, Mrs. Innes and myself, Mrs. Prendergast, with two children, Mrs. Meade with two children, Mrs. French with her husband, the Rev.—French and three children, etc.

Our escort consists of four companies of the 38th Light Infantry under Colonel Loftus,* a few soldiers of the 3rd Europeans, four light field guns belonging to the Bengal Artillery under Capt. Pearson, and a good many Sikhs and Poorbeas. Our convoy is 15 heavy guns and mortars dragged by from 20 to 32 bullocks according to their size, with a great quantity of ammunition, stores, etc. Our line of march is at least eight miles long, generally three hackeries abreast, with elephants and camels by the side of

* The 38th was I believe the first Regiment to arrive from England after the mutiny began.

the road. The mail cart finds it an excessively difficult thing to navigate through the crowd when it is unfortunate enough to meet us on the line of march.

Our marches from Agra to Mynpoorie were, 1 Omeidpoor, 2 Fyrozabad, 3 Shekoabad, 4 Ghirowl, 5 Mynpoorie.

Thursday, 28th. I met the carriage H. had sent out for me on the second day, it was a comfortable change from the dhoolie. H. has borrowed it from Capt. Evans of the 32nd, it is a very nice palkee gharie beautifully fitted up with glass windows and venetian blinds all round, and looks quite new, but it has been in the wars for there is a bullet shot through the box and another in the window and roof. Mrs. Innes shares it with me.

We get into camp so late that it is generally twelve or one before we have our tents up and breakfast ready. We were deliberating this morning about setting off before the Column; as we were going into a Cantonment (Mynpoorie) we thought there could be no danger, however, we fortunately came to the conclusion that we had better not separate ourselves from our protectors, and the first question asked us on arriving at the station, was "Have you seen anything of the enemy?" It appears that a body of them crossed the river from Rohilkund—having heard of the convoy coming from Agra—with a view of attacking it, but we could give no account of them, having seen nothing unusual on our way. However, soon after our arrival we heard heavy firing at a little distance and of course are very anxious to know the result.

The 8th Queen's Regiment is here, and the head-quarters of the 38th under Colonel Sparkes which latter join us and proceed with us to Cawnpore. Capt. Pearson with his four guns leaves us and returns for the protection of Agra; I believe, however, we shall get a couple of Royal Artillery guns instead. To pass the neighbourhood of Calpee where the rebels are in full force, appears the most perilous part of our journey.

We are to halt here for two days, and are very comfortable with all the tents up. Several visitors called. The band played in some gardens near, Mrs. Innes went to hear it, but I could not walk so far, a couple of hundred yards being the limit of my powers as yet.

Friday, 29th. Mrs. Innes and I went for a little drive through the dilapidated Cantonments; she had once stayed here with a brother, and tried in vain to find the remains of the house she occupied, everything is so changed and destroyed. The church, however, is standing and the steeple makes a desirable place for a look-out picket, which is always stationed there.

The firing we heard proceeded from Brigadier Adrian Hope's brigade, which was sent out by the Commander-in-Chief from Futteghur when he was informed that the rebels were crossing the river, in order to intercept them and prevent their reaching our column. The Brigade consists of about 200 of the 9th Lancers under Capt. Steele, some of Hodson's Horse and Capt. Remington's troop of Horse Artillery all under the command of Brigadier Adrian Hope. Capt. Steele was severely wounded, Lt. Wills attached to 9th Lancers, slightly; Major Hodson and Lt. Gough were wounded, and MacDowell second in command mortally. Thus it was a very severe engagement and it was well for us that our small force had nothing to do with it.

The Commander-in-Chief is supposed to be waiting at Futteghur until enough troops are ready to invest Oude properly, before he begins operations there.

[*February*, 1858.]

Cawnpore, Sunday, 7th. We left Mynpoorie on the 30th ult. A march or two out of it the road from Futteghur joins this one, and we encamped just at the junction. I was much disappointed to hear that the 9th Lancers had passed only a few hours before our arrival, and were encamped three miles ahead of us, with the Commander-in-Chief whom they are escorting by forced marches to Cawnpore. Almost all the troops are leaving Futteghur and are ordered to concentrate at Cawnpore. It is thought to be a great pity to leave all this Doab unprotected and open to the rebels, who have only just to cross the Ganges from Rohilkund and lay waste the whole district. There is also a large rebel force in the fort of Calpee. One night I was rather frightened, hearing a great deal of noise and commotion in camp, our tent was the outside one with only a sentry between us and the road. I got up and put on my clothes; however, after listening a little while all seemed quiet again and I went back to bed. We used to talk a good deal of what we should, could or ought to do in the event of a night attack, but I do not think we came to any very good conclusion; for myself, I almost wished that we might be attacked just for the excitement of the thing, not indeed that I had any desire to be murdered in my bed—of course we should have had the best of it—however, on the whole, I am very glad it did not happen, although, it was not an unlikely thing, for when we were encamped near the river, the rebels, consisting of five regiments under the Nana Sahib (it was said) were encamped on the opposite side, and our outlying pickets occasionally exchanged shots with the rebel sentinels. This was the case for three successive days, as the mutineers marched when we marched, halted when we halted, and pitched their camp opposite ours. Afterwards we were told that the Nana had crossed the river in the disguise of a Sepoy, and joined the force at Calpee.

As we neared Cawnpore we were pretty safe having a large column one march a-head, and another the same distance in our rear. One day Capt. Peel passed us on the line of march on a little pony, he rode like a sailor.

On Sundays the Rev.—French (a clergyman from Agra who is accompanying his wife and children to Calcutta on their way to England) used to read the service in his own tent in the evening, several of the Officers attended, and more would have done so had it been more generally known.

Sunday, 7th. We reached Cawnpore early this morning and pitched our tents in the Hotel compound. I saw Brigadier Inglis very soon, but he could give me no hope of getting on to Allahabad for three or four days; there were only three horses on the road, he would not say why they were wanted, but we soon guessed that the Commander-in-Chief (Sir Colin Campbell) was going down to have an interview with the Governor-General (Lord Canning) who is now at Allahabad.

Brigadier Inglis kindly telegraphed to H. to tell him I had arrived, and I got one or two messages from him in the course of the day, telling me to come on directly by any means, but I cannot do so.

Lady Outram has very kindly pressed me to remain with her till I go, which I am extremely glad to do instead of living by myself in the Hotel.

Monday, 8th. The 9th Lancers have gone on, I believe,

towards Lucknow, so I have again missed them. Mrs. Innes and I went out on an elephant, we passed right through the huge camp some miles in length, we saw some pickets of Highland Regiments in full costume, at the height from which we viewed them they looked exactly like toy soldiers; numbers of jolly tars were sauntering along amusing themselves; they looked so good-tempered and merry, I could hardly help smiling in their faces.

It was a pretty sight going through that extensive canvas town, built with such precision and military regularity, the vast bazaars and stores of goods—everything in fact to supply the wants of such a multitude; then the number of camels, bullock-hackeries, etc., etc., waiting, and ready at any moment to convey that town to any distance. In one day all this might be gone, and nothing but a solitary plain where it stood. What a difference between an English and an Indian camp!

Young Outram went out to Alumbagh to see his father; Lady Outram hardly liked his exposing himself to the danger, but how could he pass so close without going to see him? so he went.

I received a letter from my cousin, Charlie Pickering. I had been looking out for him the whole way, but not knowing to what battery of the Royal Artillery he belonged I could not learn anything about him. He is with General Frank's column in Oude, so I am sorry to say I shall not see him. He heard of me through Mrs. Innes' husband who is also with that column.

Tuesday, 9th. By great favor, I, and two other ladies are allowed to start this evening for Allahabad. We were told we could only have two carriages between us all—Mrs. Prendergast, two children and Ayah, Mrs. Meade, two children and Ayah, and myself, how could we spend a night and half a day in such a confined space ! By great good luck, however, and by paying well for it, I got a carriage to myself.

Mr. Eckford of the Engineers accompanied Mrs. Innes and myself on an elephant to see the remains of Cawnpore: How desolate and ruined it was. We saw the well which has been bricked up, the sepulchre of so many unfortunate people, also the assembly rooms, dreadfully battered and dilapidated. The room where all the ladies and children were massacred is no longer standing; it was I believe knocked down by our fire when the enemy held Cawnpore for the second time, after Wyndham's disastrous battle. We then went to the old entrenched camp where our brave troops held out so long against such overpowering numbers; at the height from which we viewed it (from the top of the elephant) the ground looked almost level, but the wall no doubt has suffered from the late rains and the ditch is more filled up than at the time of the siege; the two buildings were a mass of ruins, and the new barracks, which were in the hands of the rebels, were so close it seemed wonderful how they could have been held for a single day against such odds, but the garrison were brave and driven to despair, the enemy were cowards—oh that our men could have resisted but a short time longer!

In the evening I bade good-bye to Lady Outram, and thanked her for her great kindness to me, took leave also of Mrs. Innes, and left Cawnpore at 8 p.m. Mrs. Meade and Mrs. Prendergast in two kind of open waggons with curtains, and I in a common dâk gharie. An European man was seated on the box of one of the carts and we were told to keep together. One or other of the waggons, however, at each chokee got a bad horse, or broke down from some cause or other, and remained behind, the other two then had to wait until it came up, when a horse of one of the other carriages would get refractory, and have to be waited for in its turn. And so we went on, one staying for the other, and then being waited for ourselves till at last, about 12 o'clock, when we had to remain a whole hour at one place, without any sign of Mrs. Meade's waggon (she was the one who had the European sergeant on her box) I determined to risk it and go on alone, as being my only chance of reaching Allahabad by the next day. The station is about forty miles this side of Allahabad, the train only runs once a day—about 2 p.m.—H would expect me by that train, and if I did not arrive in time for it I should be obliged to remain twenty four hours at the railway station. I found by computation that at the rate we were now travelling, we could not possibly reach it by 2 o'clock the next day. I therefore determined to go on. I was perfectly alone with only the native driver, I had but one servant and I had sent him on with the luggage to wait for me at the station—my Ayah could not be induced to venture down beyond Umballah, her native place. I now got on very well with the exception of long delays at each chokee in changing horses; at one place there were none, and my poor tired horse had to go on an additional six miles to the next chokee. I reached Futteypore about seven o'clock in the morning; the horse was taken out and the man went away to smoke leaving me quite alone. On account of the heat I had all the windows of my gharie open—they are of wood and open with hinges from the top. Presently I saw a black man—a sepoy—with his red jacket creep stealthily round the carriage, at last he came up to one window and peered at me in the most horrible manner with great protruding eyes. I turned quite sick and deadly pale, in imagination I felt myself pulled out of the carriage and horribly murdered. However I would not appear afraid and asked him in Hindoostanee as coolly as I could, what he wanted; after some hesitation he produced a book, it was for officers passing up country in command of troops to sign their names in. He must have known well enough that I was not an officer in command of troops and that I was going down, not up-country. Very probably the man had no intention of hurting me, perhaps he only wanted to frighten me—which he certainly did though I would not let him see it; perhaps he saw the two guns by my side, which I was bringing down to my husband, (they were, however, not loaded.) I shall never forgot that moment—it was but a moment—of intense fear when I thought I saw a horrible death staring me in the face; my whole life crowded on me with the most vivid reality, the thought of my friends and relations, and what they would think when they heard of my death, all passed through my mind, just as in a dream, years and events all pass in a second of time. How thankful I felt when that moment was passed! An European had been killed close here only a few days before.

Soon afterwards, the driver who had brought me on so slowly came up and asked me for "bucksheesh" as a fresh coachman was to go on from here. I refused however, to give him any, having repeatedly told him, I would only give him some if he brought me on well, and I knew that if I did not keep my word, the fresh one would not take any pains to bring me on better; and the consequence was I reached the Terminus in very good time. and gave the coachman double "bucksheesh" for having driven me so well.

A large open tent is the sole convenience for passengers. I had a chilumchee of water brought and washed my face and hands which was all I could do in public, but I longed for a bath, and a change of clothes after a dusty night's journey. An officer in command of a Sikh regiment here, came up and was exceedingly kind; he sent me milk, butter, and bread for my breakfast. Soon afterwards my husband entered the tent, he had just arrived by the train; he did not know me till I came up and spoke to him, and I thought him looking altered and ill, though perhaps hardly as much so as I expected after his attack of cholera, and all that he has gone through besides.

The train he came in caught fire, but they managed to throw out the ignited stuff and prevent the gunpowder—a quantity of which was in the train, being sent up for the troops—from exploding. Mrs. Meade and Mrs. Prendergast did not arrive until half an hour before the train started, just in time to get a hurried breakfast before leaving. I feel certain if I had remained with them we should all have been too late.

I found it very hot in the train, we were about three hours reaching Allahabad, where H. has a nice large Government tent with three rooms in it. It is in the fort, and the Governor-General and his suite are in tents close to us; we could hear the band playing while they were at dinner.

Friday, 12th. Having paid up, and given presents to all our servants except the two we take with us—a Khidmutgar and Isri the bearer—we started very early this morning to go by dâk to Benares. It is considered safer to travel here by day. We have two carriages, a very nice travelling one H. has bought for the occasion, and a common dâk gharie. Besides our two servants H. has given an European (an old soldier) who wishes to get to Calcutta, a seat in the second carriage, also as a kind of protection to ourselves, in case of anything disagreeable happening.

We stopped for breakfast at a dâk bungalow, there is a kind of wall in front of it as a barricade, mounted with two little cannons made out of the sockets of telegraph posts. We arrived at Benares late in the evening, having been twelve hours and a half on the road.

Saturday, 13th February. We stayed at Benares all day and had a great deal of trouble about our dâk which is paid for by Government, which employs a certain company; they would only allow us horses on condition that we used their gharies so we were forced to leave our comfortable travelling carriage behind, having only used it one day! We left Benares in the evening about 6 o'clock, and soon reached the river Ganges, which we crossed on a bridge of boats; the road was so uneven and bad that we were obliged to have a number of coolies to drag us across, and in some places they took out the horses as the road was so dangerous.

After travelling all night we stopped at a bungalow to breakfast; Sir Edward Lugard and Dr. McAndrew were there on their way to join the camp.

We stopped again for dinner, and then resumed our journey. We constantly meet detachments of troops marching up country some in bullock-dâk gharies and some on foot; the bungalows and outhouses are generally full of them. During the night I lost a little book of sketches, from the door of the gharie sliding open without my knowing it.

Monday, 15th. Travelled again all day and all night,

crossed the Rajmahal Hills and reached the railway station at Raneegunge (120 miles from Calcutta) in time to take a very hurried and bad breakfast at an indifferent hotel before the daily and only train started, which it does at 10 o'clock in the morning, and we reached Calcutta on the evening of the 16th, after travelling for three days and three nights without intermission, or six days and five nights from Allahabad.

The terminus is on the opposite side of the river to the town ; we crossed in a boat (there is a steam ferry) and then we each got into a palanquin, hundreds of which are waiting for hire, and went to Spence's Hotel, where we took possession of a very handsome suite of apartments on the first floor. How I did enjoy the comfortable bed and a good night's rest after so much travelling !

Sunday, February 21st. We went to the Cathedral (St. Paul's) and heard a sermon from the Bishop of Madras who I had heard preach before at the consecration of the church at Umballah. This time it was a panegyric on the late Bishop of Calcutta, on whose character and actions he preached for more than an hour; he was instrumental in building or finishing this Cathedral, which is I believe considered a handsome edifice.

Mrs. Meade and Mrs. Prendergast, who we left behind at Allahabad, arrived a few days after us and are at this hotel. Poor Mrs. Meade, who lost all her things in the flight from Gwalior, was reduced to the same condition again by her gharie taking fire, from the wheels not being sufficiently greased; she and her two children arrived in Calcutta almost destitute of clothing. I offered her everything in my power, but she had all she wanted from Mrs. Prendergast.

Monday, 22nd. Colonel Ewart, of the Highlanders, called. He is most grateful to my husband for having, as he says, saved his life. He was wounded after Lucknow, and his arm amputated which almost invariably in this campaign has proved fatal, and in his case gangrene was setting in, and I believe the doctors had given him up, when H. took him out of the hospital, brought him to his own quarters, and took care of him.

All passages to England on board the steamers are engaged for two or three months to come, so H. resolved on a bold stroke and has taken ours to Madras, for the Company is obliged by contract to keep a certain number of berths vacant for Madras and Ceylon passengers. We hope to get on somehow from Madras, but if not, we can land there and wait for another opportunity.

We had an early dinner and in the evening of the 22nd of February went on board the "Nubia" a fine ship, one of the largest I believe of the Peninsular and Oriental Company's steamers. We have a cabin with five berths in it all to ourselves. Our two servants came on board with us, and had their arrears of wages paid them, they cried bitterly at parting from us, and H. told them he should be sure to return to India and see them again before long.*

On Tuesday 23rd at daybreak we weighed anchor, dropped it again in the evening, and so on until the 26th, on which morning at 6 o'clock we left the Sandheads and reached Madras on the evening of Saturday the 27th.

Sunday, 28th. H. went on shore and saw the Gazette with his name in it as Brevet Lieut. Colonel, and in a later Gazette that he was also made Companion of the Bath. We

* He returned within the year, and they both found him out and took service with him again.

also heard of the wreck of the Ava (the P. and O. Company's steamer which left before ours) she was not in her regular course, but taking treasure to Trincomalee. The Captain not being well acquainted with the coast, she went on the rocks which abound there. Happily all the passengers were saved, but they lost all their effects. Many of them were Lucknow survivors, who had just purchased a fresh wardrobe only to lose it again. There is a Captain Mangles on board who had sent his wife home in the Ava and hoped to follow her in a few months; he was unexpectedly able to come in the next steamer. Of course he was very anxious about her and it was most provoking to be only three or four days' journey behind without her being aware of it. He told me this was the third time they had lost all their things since the mutiny began. We have four or five widows on board and almost everyone is in mourning. There is a Mrs. Dashwood, a very young widow with two little boys, the younger born during the siege; she lost her husband, her brother-in-law, and a child in Lucknow. There is also a Mrs. Radcliffe with some very pretty children.

We left Madras on Sunday afternoon the 28th February, about four o'clock. We had of course, to turn out of our cabin, but I got a berth in a very large one with two ladies, in a better part of the ship, opening out of the grand saloon.

March, 1858.

We arrived at Point de Galle late on the evening of the 2nd, and went on shore the next morning; found the hotels very full, many of the unfortunate Ava's passengers having remained here to get a few things before continuing their voyage. Finished coaling at five o'clock on Thursday, and took in a number of passengers though the ship seemed full enough before.

We anchored off Aden at 1.30 a.m., on Thursday, the 11th. We went on shore very early in the morning, and drove to Cantonments two or three miles distant. The road at first lies along the sea shore, then over a steep mountain from the top of which we looked over the Cantonment lying at its base; it is quite surrounded by hills, and looks as if built in the mouth of a gigantic crater, nothing could exceed the desolate appearance of the place, and yet it had a look of grandeur.

We drove up to the best Inn in the place; there was only one room, common to every one, and the nearest approach to a breakfast that we could get was some lemonade and a few biscuits. We just saw the famous Turkish Wall at a distance, and then returned to the shore where we made the best breakfast we could out of the remnants the other passengers had left. However we had had a cool drive, and I felt glad that we had gone so early when I saw those who had breakfasted first and gone to the Cantonment after, come back looking so hot and jaded.

We returned to the ship at one o'clock, for there was only an open verandah to sit in, exposed to the hot wind and clouds of dust; the dining room was in constant request so we could not sit there, and the bedrooms, that a few were fortunate enough to get, were mere cabins, small and dark. However, we were not much better off on board ship, for coal dust is even more disagreeable than common dust or sand, and the whole place was in a dreadful condition, every chair and bench perfectly black, everything you touched sooty, the eatables were the same and served up on an uncommonly dirty tablecloth. The cabins were insufferable from the heat and closeness consequent on the port-holes being kept shut, and even that fails to keep out the enemy entirely; clean bedding is absolutely necessary after a day's coaling. A large supply is taken in here, sufficient to last to Suez and back, as it is terribly dear there, on account of the difficult passage and length of time sailing vessels take with their freight of coals to go up the Red Sea.

We weighed anchor at five, in order to pass through the somewhat dangerous straits by daylight. I remained late on deck enjoying the wild, strange-looking scenery of these parts.

Friday, 12th. Last night H. and all the passengers forward on this side of the ship, were washed out of their beds. The captain I believe luffed the ship and the waves struck her. I was on the same side but near the stern, so escaped the wetting but the dead lights were put in. The sea is very rough here and makes me feel very uncomfortable, we also feel the heat very much, it always is hot in the Red Sea, I believe, and in consequence of the roughness of the weather, we are obliged to keep our port almost constantly shut, which is very trying but necessary, for this morning I went into my cabin just in time to see a wave dash into my bed which is just under the port-hole, and another day I was awakened by a dash of spray in my face.

Sunday, 14th. The Captain read prayers having a flag spread over the capstan to form a reading desk. The ship rolled so much it was very difficult to stand, and after I had twice been deposited in my low chair by a violent lurch, I thought it prudent to remain there during the remainder of the service.

Wednesday, 17th. We passed close to some land and at

night reached Suez; we were obliged, however, to anchor a good way off. Very busy drawing lots to determine who should go in the first caravan across the desert, and who in the second. We have drawn the first, and know not whether to be glad or sorry, time will shew.

Thursday, 18th March. We took a very early breakfast, and having seen our luggage in, and well feed the steward and stewardess, we seated ourselves in a small steamer, or flat, for there is not water enough for large steamers to get up to Suez. We were about an hour on the voyage, sitting as close as we could pack on the open deck, without cover or awning, however, it was early, and we did not suffer from the heat, indeed, we found it rather cold than otherwise. When we landed, having made up our party of six, we proceeded to choose a likely-looking van from among twelve or thirteen standing in a row; bought some delicious oranges to assuage our thirst during our journey across "the desert," and in due course of time, after some difficulty in harnessing the two mules and two horses to their respective vans, we set off, but were not allowed to go far, for first one van would break down, and then another, or their steeds would refuse to move, and the whole caravan had to wait, for we were not allowed to separate ourselves for fear of being robbed and plundered by the Arabs. Presently our turn came, and after being detained by the misfortunes of others, our horses kicked, plunged and reared, and for some time could not be persuaded to proceed. It was a curious thing to see our cavalcade rushing along helter-skelter (generally at full gallop) anywhere, following no road, some taking most eccentric courses over huge stones and through deep ruts. Formerly there was something of a road or track, when the whole journey was performed in this way, but now that the greater part is by train, this is merely the way to the nearest point where the railway is finished, and consequently is constantly changing as the line progresses. The jolting was really terrible; poor Mr. Graham Birch suffered dreadfully, he is a very young officer who had gone out to a Bengal Cavalry regiment, but never joined it, as on his arrival it was in open mutiny; he was severely wounded while serving with Havelock's force.

What with the halts and changing horses, we were nearly six hours going 18 or 20 miles to the point where the train was drawn up (I cannot call it a station the train seemed to have stopped there by chance) and with great difficulty room was found for us, either in first or second class carriages, lucky enough to get into either, and difficult enough too, for it seemed more like mounting to the deck of a large ship, than the usual easy transit from a platform to, the carriage—they were comfortable when we got there and I was fortunate enough to get a first class one.

After going a short distance we came to some tents where we stopped to have dinner—as it was called—but I never before sat down to such a disgusting meal. To the best of my recollection there was no tablecloth, some hard, tough, dark-looking legs of mutton (they were intended for) a few wretched half starved chickens with hard biscuit (no bread) some cheese, and a few plates of sliced orange formed the repast, and I have no doubt that there was plenty of it left for the next batch of passengers, as it was impossible to eat much of it. After waiting a couple of hours, we proceeded by train to Cairo which we reached about dusk. The outward bound passengers were here, so we had great difficulty in getting Hotel room, however, we were able to find rooms in the third Hotel we drove to, and we all dined at the table d' hôte.

Friday, 19th March. All the passengers started again at four this morning. We stayed behind, and intend remaining a few days in Egypt, and to go on by another and less crowded steamer.

The second party which left the ship at Suez, in which there were a number of children, had a more fatiguing journey than we had. They were not able to come into the city of Cairo at all, as they reached it in the middle of the night and had to leave the first thing in the morning, they therefore remained at the railway station. They did not get on in the vans even as well as we did, for I heard they only had our tired horses.

After breakfast we went to Sheppard's Hotel in which there was then plenty of room, and we had a nice drawing-room with a piano in it. H. hired a Dragoman, but I do not think they are of much use.

Saturday, 20th. We started for the Pyramids taking our luncheon with us. H. and the Dragoman each had a donkey, and I a kind of chair without wheels between two donkeys, one in front and one behind, under the impression that it would be less fatiguing than riding, but it was quite the reverse, certainly, a more uncomfortable and painful conveyance I was never in, but I was determined to go, cost me what it would. We went two or three miles through old Cairo, before we came to the river, where my chair had to be taken down, and put into a boat, and very glad I was of the respite from the dreadful jolting of my conveyance.

After going some distance on the other side of the Nile,

we came to a broad plain or desert, from whence the Pyramids looked so grand and stately; in front of them is a small hill over which the Sphinx* peers, and looks exactly as if he were keeping guard over the Pyramids, Long before we got close to these wonders we were assailed by numbers of Arabs, all clamouring to be engaged to shew us over them. When we arrived at the base of the first one, I descended from my chair, and although I could not walk a hundred yards on plain ground without great fatigue, I resolved if possible to get to the top. I therefore told four or five Arabs to pull me up, without any effort of my own. These Pyramids are composed of huge blocks of stone piled one on the top of the other, forming gigantic steps from one to three feet high, (the height of the largest Pyramid is nearly 500 feet) my arms were nearly pulled out of their sockets, but I got up at last, resting several times on the way. The view from the top was very singular, a narrow strip of green, looking just like a ribbon, showed where the Nile flowed, and all the rest was desert. As I sat on the summit at that great height with the Arabs jabbering their own (and to me unknown) language round us, it seemed to me as if I were living in ages long past, and I felt a great disinclination to break the spell, and begin the descent. Presently the guides came up to us, and began to be extortionate, wanting us to give them money, otherwise, they said they would not take us down, and that we were entirely at their mercy. I must confess I felt a little uncomfortable, we seemed so much cut off from the rest of the world, but H. carried things with a high hand, said they should not have anything till we were at the bottom, so at last they consented to conduct us there. The descent was

* It was pointed out to me that the Sphinx was a female, the Grecian Sphinx was undoubtedly feminine, but must not be confounded with the Egyptian Sphinx which is masculine.

even more fatiguing than the ascent, and for a person at all prone to giddiness it would have been very fearful to look down from such a vast height. After eating our luncheon we just took a look at the mortuary chamber, in the body of the Pyramid, but did not feel at all inclined to penetrate its gloomy interior.

It was bad enough coming, but I did not know how to support the journey back, the jolting of my conveyance was so dreadful, and I arrived at the Hotel more dead than alive.

There is such a funny old maid here, who travels about a great deal by herself, or sometimes with friends, she took a great fancy to me, and used to talk a great deal to us at meal times. Rested on Sunday, and on Monday morning the 23rd of March, we left Cairo. We had heard nothing of our luggage since we left the steamer and had given it up for lost, but fortunately it arrived in time. We had been much inconvenienced by the want of it, having only a small bag with us, H. had been obliged to buy a couple of shirts and miserable calico things they were. During our journey by train we were much struck by the high dove-cotes which form the most prominent feature in all the villages we passed. At noon we stopped for refreshments, and found them far superior to what we had had before in the desert. Afterwards we proceeded on foot a short distance to the banks of the Nile, and there had to wait some little time for the steamer to take us across. A fine bridge is in process of erection, and when that and the whole line of railway is finished the journey across the desert will be a mere bagatelle* The approach to Alexandria by train is very pretty, along the edge of the water, on the surface of

* There was no idea at that time of a canal, but in 1863 on our way home from Ceylon we travelled in the same steamer with M. de Lesseps, who gave my husband a copy of the plan of the projected Suez Canal.

which we observed some very curious optical delusions. The terminus is a long distance from the town. We rode in a very large kind of omnibus to the Peninsular and Oriental Hotel, but found it full, so went on to the Hôtel d' Europe.

Tuesday, 23rd March. H. has taken our passage to Marseilles in a French steamboat—the Simoïs. We rose very early and had great difficulty in getting our passport in such a hurry. We drove down to the Quay about eleven o'clock, a *Commissionaire* insisted on getting on the box to help us with our things, although we had only three small trunks (having sent the remainder of our luggage by the Southampton route) H. told the man he did not want him and should give him nothing. On arriving at the Quay twenty Arabs crowded round us to take our luggage, and there was such a scramble, in the middle of which the *Commissionaire* while assisting, suddenly overbalanced himself, and he and the box came tumbling into the body of the carriage—an open one—where I was sitting alone, H. having fortunately just gone out, how he escaped I hardly know, but neither the man nor I were hurt. Then came another trouble with the boatmen, however, we ended that by jumping into the nearest boat. H. gave a rupee to the *Commissionaire* and another to the porters, and we put off to the ship; it was not till some time after we got on board that H. discovered he had lost his great coat which was last seen in the care of the importunate *Commissionaire*, so we gave four shillings for the transit of three small boxes, a few yards with the loss af a good great coat into the bargain—this is a specimen of the expenses of travelling.

We weighed anchor about two o'clock, and soon got into rough water, the effects of the late storm; for two days I was very ill and could not leave my bed. I was never so ill before at sea. We arrived at Malta late at night on the 26th, and anchored in the Lazaretto Harbour.

There are several English passengers on board, among them the Rev.—Owen, vicar of Yoxford in Suffolk, with his wife and nephew, John Enys, they have been to the Holy Land, and up the Nile on a tour of pleasure. I was showing our book of photographs to Mr. Enys, amongst them was one of Dorchester, and it turned out that he was present when that identical picture was taken, he at that time being a pupil of the Rev.—Moule, living in the next house to ours in Dorchester in 1854!

We are very comfortable on board the "Simoïs," have a good cabin to ourselves, and find everything very good on board, the only drawback is the dirty state of the deck, and the sailors look different from English ones; but I must say the table is infinitely better kept than in an English steamer.

Monday, 29th March. Up at six to see the Islands of Corsica and Sardinia between which we passed, the sea being smooth enough to allow of our doing so, instead of taking the usual course round the Islands.

Tuesday, 30th. We arrived at Marseilles very early this morning. We had little difficulty at the Custom House, H. was merely asked if he had any tobacco, and paid five francs for two and a half pounds of Latakia. We went to the Hotel, and were joined there by the Owens. Poor Mr. Owen was in great trouble, the officer on board the steamer whose duty it is to take charge of the passports, had left his at Malta. He had therefore to go all over the town to get a new one, have it viséed, etc., pay a good sum of money, and only reached the Hotel in time to get a hurried breakfast before starting by train.

We turned off the direct line and visited Nîmes to see the celebrated Roman antiquities there.

We stayed a few days in Paris, and H had an interview with the Ambassador—Lord Cowley. We arrived in England on the 9th of April 1858, after an absence of three years and four months.